PELICAN BOOKS

THE FUTURE OF RELIGION

Kathleen Bliss read history and then theology at
Cambridge, taught in the Midlands and London,
married and went to India for seven years. She
edited a fortnightly journal (*Christian News-
Letter*) for an international readership for five years
and organized debates between Christians, Human-
ists and others for the B.B.C. She was General
Secretary of the Church of England Board of
Education, 1958–67, and was associated with the
World Council of Churches from 1948 to 1968,
travelling all over the world in the interests of
religion and education. Kathleen Bliss is now
Lecturer in Religious Studies at the University of
Sussex.

KATHLEEN BLISS

The Future of Religion

Centre for
Faith and Spirituality
Loughborough University

PENGUIN BOOKS

Penguin Books Ltd, Harmondsworth, Middlesex, England
Penguin Books Inc., 7110 Ambassador Road, Baltimore, Maryland 21207, U.S.A.
Penguin Books Australia Ltd, Ringwood, Victoria, Australia

—

First published by C. A. Watts & Co. 1969
Published in Pelican Books 1972

—

Copyright © Kathleen Bliss, 1969

—

Made and printed in Great Britain
by Hazell Watson & Viney Ltd,
Aylesbury, Bucks
Set in Monotype Bembo

To Michael
Lucy and Victoria

CONTENTS

PREFACE

AN eminent American sociologist, Professor Milton Yinger, has written the following, which might be taken as a verdict of lunacy on a writer who, having read his words, then ventures on a book with a title such as this one bears:

> Few would deny that an attempt to give a conclusive statement regarding the future of religion would be foolhardy indeed; there are too many different opinions, too much controversial evidence, for a definite statement. One consideration, however, may throw some light on the problem. Nothing stands out more clearly in the study of religious phenomena than the extreme variability and adaptability of religion on the one hand, accompanied, on the other, by a basic similarity which underlies various expressions.

A 'conclusive statement' is far from my intention. I believe that religion has a future for (among others) the reasons that Professor Yinger states, but I am no believer in the existence, or the possibility, of some essence of all religion, or religion-as-such. What is common to all religions is, in my view, people and their needs. All beliefs are held, all institutions created, by human beings, and they in their turn receive from these a part of the material that helps to make distinctive cultures.

The 'crisis of religion' often spoken of today is of western origin, caused by the changes roughly described in such phrases as 'the industrial revolution', 'the development of science and technology', and so on. I have lived a part of my life in rural India, in a culture formed by a different religion, and from this viewpoint have seen something of the changes that are made in people's lives as western industrialization spreads and the developments in science and technology are applied to public health, education and communications. This is not a book about the future of all religions in all or even most of the senses in which that word is used, which I roughly sketch in my first chapter. My interest is in religion caught in the developing present which is becoming the unknown future, a future in which ideas and institutions formed mainly in the west become increasingly the dynamic forces of the whole world and meet perhaps their challenge from certain forgotten needs of men and from yet unperceived needs of the future. I see the possibility that the alternative to a development of religion could be a massive growth of superstition. That men who value reason should take religion seriously enough to be concerned about its future seems to me important in realms beyond the narrow confines of religious institutions.

It is not possible to talk about the future of religion without referring at many points to the course it has thus far run. Even the most personal of faiths owes much to tradition and the most eccentric of sects is usually a criticism of institutional religion. I have not organized this book on historical lines: I am well aware of the strictures of Professor Karl Popper on projection into the future of lines that can be traced in the past. I have begun with what is most visible in religion, its buildings, and finished with what is most invisible, the object of faith which men have called God.

1 *September* 1968   KATHLEEN BLISS

ACKNOWLEDGEMENTS

I SHOULD like to thank many colleagues and friends who have knowingly or unknowingly contributed to this book by informing or challenging its author, and more specifically Mr T. M. Schuller of the publishers for firm and patient pressure, Miss M. A. Bryan for working on the manuscript, and Miss Dorothy Barsby for producing for the printer a typescript out of what she was too kind to describe as a handful of pieces of paper.

K. B.

I

WHAT IS RELIGION?

WHAT is religion? This is one of those questions to which people will give a wide variety of answers varying with their experience of life – how they were brought up, what they have seen, heard or read, where they have been, what life has done to them as persons. But whether they are for it or against it, whether they think it true or false or are uncertain or indifferent, people yet believe that the word 'religion' identifies for them something that is or was.

And will be? That is another matter. Before the future can be discussed *what it is* that might or might not have a future has to be in some sense defined. Among the innumerable answers to the question 'What is religion?' there are at least some groupings. I distinguish four, and these will be the subject-matter of this book.

Religion as Systems of Religious Thought

First then systems of religious thinking and belief: 'isms' such as Hinduism, Buddhism – 'the world's great religions' as people would say. Even if there were no believers or practitioners of them these could still be described from their literature, architecture and other visible evidence. Comparative religion deals mainly with religion in this sense and the very phrase implies that something can be compared with something else.

My school atlas contained a map 'showing the distribution of the chief religions of the world'. (I regret that I cannot remember what Africa looked like.) At the bottom was a table of numbers of Buddhists, Hindus, Shintoists, Christians,

Mohammedans. Jews did not figure on the map, but were present in the table. China was allotted to Confucianism (which counted as a religion for such purposes) and there was a misty tailing-off into small groups for whom there was not much room on the map.

The whole idea on which this map was based is a modern and a western one. 'Buddhism' was not invented or used by the followers of Buddha, nor 'Judaism' by Jews, still less 'Mohammedanism' by followers of Mohammed. 'Shintoism' is an impossible term to translate into Japanese. All these names were imposed by others in an attempt to understand the faith of other men from the outside; to grasp religion as systems was part of the European passion for classifying and analysing. But as Professor E. E. Evans-Pritchard the distinguished anthropologist of African religion points out, analysis involves abstracting from context and this both illuminates and falsifies. W. Cantrell-Smith speaks of the 'reification' or 'thingifying' of religion by the modern western mind in order to get a grasp of it. We have been dominated by this way of looking at 'religions' until by now we have taken from it what can be learned. Some at least of modern scholars, in contrast with those whose eager collecting of data pigeonholed men's faiths as 'systems', try to understand faith as those who hold faith understand it, in its infinite complexity and continual movement.

This means also that the solid blocks of colour on the map have to be seen as dappled and diversified. It was a long time before I realized – by living among them – that for Indian villagers who appeared as 'Hindu' on the map local gods and shrines and the spirits of trees and water were much more truthfully their religion than the Hindu pantheon: that astrology and divination, charms and nostrums persisted even among the educated while the study of Hindu scriptures and philosophy was the pursuit only of the few.

All 'the world's great religions' in fact show in one way or another a *gap* between the teachings and writings of their great exponents on the one hand (be they writers, leaders, teachers or saints) and the mass of the people on the other. That the gap is absolute is far from true. Whole peoples have been, over the centuries, deeply affected by particular religions. The affirmatives and negatives of a religion affect temperament and outlook, predisposing men to attitudes of fatalism or to assertiveness as well as to specific actions and taboos: its organizational patterns may be indistinguishable from society itself, as the caste system has been for centuries part and parcel of Hinduism and the Christian parish was the local social and administrative unit of western Europe. The rhythm imposed on life by religious festivals, be they weekly Sabbaths or Sundays, or seasonal events, is visible in every culture. The gap may be narrowed from the other side also: popular needs press upon high religion and bring about modifications of dogma, moral standards and ritual practices.

The existence of a gap is sometimes ignored. For example, how many of those who talk about the Middle Ages as 'the ages of faith' realize how much of pagan beliefs and practices, including sorcery, witchcraft and fertility rites, still continued from Europe's pre-Christian past, or what prodigious effort went into teaching, persuading or compelling men to make of Christianity a religion of everyday life? Man has to live. The first claim on time and energy has always been the struggle to survive against nature and against enemies. He has also to live with the given realities of the human condition – birth and death, childhood, adolescence and senescence; relations with others as kin, as neighbours, as strangers; relations with himself and the warring emotions within. He seeks from religion what will enable him to live.

But what have become the great religions are not the faiths that make men feel cosy in the natural world: they are those that have beckoned them on towards achievements of thought or imagination or action beyond immediate grasp. Men will resort to magic under stress or to superstition in ignorance but the great religions have been carried to their high position not by simpletons and knaves but by men – individuals and small groups – endowed with intelligence and sensitivity, moral insight and courage. It is this mark of genius upon them at their source and at the points of refreshment along the line of their historical development that constitutes their claim to greatness and not their spread on the map or their statistics of adherents.

Religion as 'Organized Religion'

'Religion' also means the immediately visible forms of churches and temples, sacred acts and persons set apart to perform them. Scholars of religions certainly study institutions and would take in this second meaning of the word under the first. But if we are discussing popular usages as well as scholarly ones then 'organized religion' merits separate treatment.

'Organized religion' is what stands in the gap mentioned in the previous section and tries to close it. Temples and churches exist for worshippers and invite their active participation in religious practices that derive (wholly or in part) from the teachings, sacraments and forms of a religious tradition. Priests, ministers, pastors, religious teachers, evangelists – all in a multitude of ways stir people up to take religion more seriously, or to accept belief, or to change beliefs already held.

The professional leadership which has emerged in relation to all 'organized religion' is never popular for long anywhere. Fear and suspicion of priestly power is world-wide and well-founded. The noblest teachings of religion have not prevented the abuse of power by some of those who mediate divine mysteries to men, nor the accumulation of wealth by institutions, nor the deadening weight of custom, nor the inflexibility of bureaucracy. Hence the upheavals that in the name of reform have divided most religions into sects, or have reconstituted organization, or ejected those in power in favour of others. Tight hierarchical structures are open to one sort of abuse; democratic ones to another. Protest movements against organized religion frequently turn into new religious organizations.

So the man who invests his life in the service of organized religion starts as the inheritor of a long tradition of wariness towards it on the part of those he wants to influence and serve. But the suspicion is in part compounded of disappointment: 'things ought to be otherwise' and the willingness of men to struggle to make them so has given new life to institutions many times over. Can this happen again?

Organized religion is a proper field of study for the sociologist. We have census figures, national opinion polls, mass observation studies. These have been directed to estimating church attendance, opinions on religious education in schools and general opinions on belief either among a national sample or among special groups (sixth-formers, university students, certain industrial workers, for example). They tell us what people think about organized religion but leave unanswered the question how much they know about what they have opinions upon.

What we lack are enough closely observed studies of religious institutions: what sort of people belong to them; what they do; how authority is distributed and used; where money comes from and goes to; what the relationships are with the local community and a host more facts. Opinion is no substitute for study. On the other hand organized religion has so strong a historical dimension that what the sociologist sees is not the whole story. Organized religion is always living with or living down or living up to, its own past.

Religion as 'My Religion'

The third general meaning of religion in popular use is obviously the most widely diversified. One use of the phrase may not be in any conflict or contrast with organized religion or with the first definition of religion given above. 'He takes his religion seriously' usually means 'he is regular in religious observance' or 'he tries to make his way of life conform to the religion he accepts' or 'he applies himself to learning more about the religion he professes'. There are many such people in all religions. There are traditional ways of expressing such commitment: the Mohammedan shopkeeper scrapes and saves for half a life time to make the pilgrimage to Mecca; the Hindu travels to Benares or Tanjore: the evangelical Christian goes to a convention or a Billy Graham campaign. There are also many new ways of making the religion one belongs to a matter of personal commitment in faith and action and these are becoming more important in the religious picture as social conformity declines.

Sometimes the search for a solution to their own problems makes individuals agents of wider changes in religious beliefs, customs and institutions. All religions have such persons in their histories: they often founded religious groups or communities; many such individuals have had their greatest influence after their death.

Next one can consider a small number of individuals each remarkable in a particular way. Unable to accept wholly the doctrines of religion as taught and the constrictions of religious organization on individual thought they yet find religious questions of overpowering importance to them intellectually and spiritually; or they may take a moral stand which they can only justify on grounds that are fundamentally religious. These men and women are all characterized by a sense of the urgent necessity to find a new faith or to reinterpret an old one in such a way that it does not ask them either to abandon the modern world or to accept it on its own terms. Their influence is mainly in what they write. They appeal to a thoughtful audience that shares their starting point. Søren Kierkegaard, the father of modern existentialism, is perhaps the most outstanding example of the individual who protests against religious organization that has become totally stultifying to the individual spirit. He did it in a way incomprehensible to his contemporaries but of immense stimulus after his death, both in religion and in philosophy. In this century one can speak of Dietrich Bonhoeffer, Simone Weil, Teilhard de Chardin, Martin Buber among the many who have spoken as individuals to individuals through their writings. The humanist concern to re-interpret religion in non-theistic and evolutionary terms is represented by Julian Huxley.

Lastly there are those – probably a very large number – who regard religion as a personal matter in the sense that one man's opinion is as good as another's. This individualism is primarily a phenomenon of modern civilization with its mobility and rootlessness. Whatever their religious affiliation may have been most people tend to abandon it when they move from one place to another, especially if they move from rural area or small town to city. This much at least is sociologically verifiable by census figures and by studies done in the United States and tested elsewhere.

But what do all these individuals *really* believe? Far more inquiry would be needed (and a far clearer definition of what is being inquired into than most inquiries of the opinion-poll type have worked with) before that question could be answered. One sees some trends: belief in immortality in the sense of life-after-death is declining and belief in (or a hazarding of the possibility of) transmigration of souls seems to be on the increase. Some types of 'my religion' have a good deal of superstition in them; many seem to qualify for inclusion in David Riesman's description of personal neuroses elevated to the dignity of a religion (inside organized religion, surely, as well as outside?). Would psychologists generally support Elliott Slater's view that beliefs and personality modify each other till they fit like hand and glove – which is to say in effect that there are as many patterns of believing and behaving as there are people, no two believing in just the same way?

In England opinion polls have shown that the majority of people think they believe in God. Ninety per cent want religious education for their children in schools. Even more surprisingly, more than half the sixth-formers want to keep religious teaching in school in spite of radical criticisms.[1] David Martin says that the Englishman's religion comprises 'a preference for "decency" as distinct from mere forms and practices and a veneration for the person of Christ'.[1] Recent inquiries in the United States have not disclosed among many *church-goers* a greater content to religious belief than this. One is forced to ask whether the 'religious organization-men' perhaps exaggerate the differences of belief inside and outside organized religion in the conditions of today. There is no possibility of compelling the young along the channels of religious belief accepted by their fathers: a world of choice is open to them and their protest to adults comes ever more insistently, 'let us choose for ourselves your world is not ours'

[1] EDWIN COX, *Sixth Form Religion* (S.C.M. Press, 1967).

[2] DAVID MARTIN, *A Sociology of English Religion* (Heinemann and S.C.M. Press, 1967).

The End of Religion

The most radical alternative to a future of religion is total denial that it has any future at all, either as organized religion, or as a system of beliefs, or as personal faith. Those who take this view include religious pessimists and secular optimists, who both consider that they are making the only possible deductions from observable facts. Their observations would include on the one hand the decline of religious observance and the weakness of religious institutions in society as many of their erstwhile functions are taken over by the state or other agencies. On the other hand they would say that there is an observable decay of belief. As already said, belief is more difficult to assess than, for example, church-going and those who observe a decline of belief would point to the many factors in life which used to be given a religious explanation and now do not demand one. If people do not *need* to believe in religion then one appears to be justified in predicting that in time they will not do so.

But an end of religion is not only a conclusion from some observable facts: it is a kind of myth and this makes it far more powerful than prediction from observation. The myth is current in several different forms and each one is associated with a myth about the beginnings of religion. In his *Future of an Illusion* Freud wrote that, as men realized that the desire for a God was the longing of weak and defenceless human beings for an almighty father and that as they admitted that their religion was wishful thinking, it would die away. But Freud had also written in *Totem and Taboo* about the origins of religion. He postulated an uprising of sons against an autocratic father who kept all the women of the tribe for himself. The sons, according to Freud, murdered the father and thereafter assuaged their guilt for this, the first parricide, by engaging in the totemic feast in which they ate the totem animal. In this Freud saw the origins of sacraments.[1] When his theory was attacked, Freud said (in *The Death of an Illusion*) that he was not speaking of all religion but of totemic religion. But this is just what could not stand up to the facts known to ethnologists and anthropologists. Totemism arrived on the religious scene late in history and sacrifice early; totemic tribes do not, except in extremely rare examples, eat the totemic animal at all. Exploded by scientists, yet *Totem and Taboo* goes on being published and read and his theories about wishful thinking, based in large part on observations of patients, are still current. Why? Freud's reputation as an analyst and skill as a writer may partly account for this. But the myth corresponds, like other myths, to a reality: in this case the widespread wish that religion were dead.

The second source of myth about the origins and death of religion comes from Marx. Religion, wrote Marx, was 'the sigh of the oppressed creature, the heart of a heartless world, the spirit of soulless stagnation, the opium of the people'. It was Lenin who reinterpreted Marx's words with a venomous hatred of religion. For Marx religion would disappear with the conditions that give rise to it: a classless society would not need it. One can see many traces of the influence of this attitude even outside communist countries and among non-Marxists, for it adds a general theory of the function of religion to the accusations of exploitation and obscurantism made against it by summoning historical evidence and generalizing from it.

The third type of myth is the evolutionary. Again the origins and the expected end of religion are connected. Religion emerges with the earliest traces of human thought and communal activity. A philosopher like Suzanne Langer for example suggests that the origins of language may have

---

[1] Mercia Eliade examines the case for this statement in an essay in Vol. 1 of *Studies in Religion* (University of Chicago Press, 1968).

been in ritual: others see in religion early forms of conceptual thinking and of social organization. Thus religion is recognized as of very great importance to man in his early stages of development. Ideas of virtually inevitable progress which were, at the turn of the century, enthusiastically read into the 'evolutionary' story of man's development, have now no supporters. But the belief that man has himself become responsible for the course of his own evolution has put the human mind in a position that it has never before occupied in man's thought about himself. No particular name can be attached to this widespread generalized conception of religion as essentially part of man's early history which he leaves behind him with his past and which is unthinkable as part of his destiny as the director of his own evolution. Some sort of replacement of past forms of religion by a contemplation of the mystery of the processes and wonders of nature is suggested by Julian Huxley[1] and others.

The feeling that religion is near its end, having come with man from his beginnings and through some stages of intense intellectual activity, is in the air. Oddly enough it is often believers who seem most affected by what they breathe while a man like Kingsley Martin (in *Objections to Humanism*)[2] who makes no bones about wanting to see the end of religion is impressed by its toughness. Humanists are divided; they usually shy away from the idea that humanism itself might be cast in any of the roles of religion and most particularly from the idea of a humanist orthodoxy or establishment. Some at least of them envisage a continuance of religious thought and action and sharpening of their own perceptions against those of religion. Other humanists however seem to believe that humanism will only develop when religion is off the scene.

[1] *Religion without Revelation* (Watts, London, 1967).
[2] *Objections to Humanism*, ed. H. J. BLACKHAM (Constable & Co., 1964).

If there is truth in an old generalization that more civilizations perish from decay within than from attack by external enemies, and if this can be applied to religion, then it might be possible to pose the question whether the end of religion is not more in the hands of its believers and supporters than of its enemies? If they are captured by myths and prophecies of the end of religion they will be more powerful to bring it about than any opponents of religion could be. If on the other hand they believe that religion belongs not only to the start of man's journey but is a living road towards the achievement of man's full humanity, they will not be turned away from making the changes that response to such a challenge will make necessary.

II

BUILDINGS: FROM THE PAST TO THE PRESENT

ALL over the world religion impinges on the eye as buildings. No one needs to be an antiquarian, an architect or even a believer to recognize a mosque, a temple or a church. Their shape, the age of most of them, the symbols that decorate them, the unlikeness to other buildings around them may all provide clues to their identity. But they are recognized also because they are part of a cultural inheritance: they offer the distinctiveness of being religious buildings and yet they exercise a profound influence on the style of other buildings just as sacred texts have helped to form literary style. Even if they are new, they stand in a certain tradition that familiarity enables us to recognize. Chartres is identifiable in Coventry Cathedral.

For the most part we are the inheritors of one main tradition of religious buildings. If we live at the confluence of cultures we may be surrounded by the buildings of two or three different religions. Alexandria, till Nasser came, had been for many centuries a city of Arabs, Jews and Greeks and therefore of mosques, synagogues and churches: a city unique in the world for the length of its mixed religious history.

But what used to be rare is now becoming common. Wherever there is cultural mixture accompanied by tolerance the skyline proclaims the fact. The onion towers of Orthodox churches appear today above the wheat of the Canadian prairie or on the savannah of Brazil. Buddhist shrines are being built by former outcaste villagers in India, where Buddhism has not been at home for centuries. A Mormon temple towers up in a South Kensington street. Mobility, migration, the settling of refugee populations in new lands, create cultural and religious mixtures not known before. Rural people moving into towns, immigrants trying to find a place to belong, and city dwellers irked by the ineffectiveness of the religious institutions they find around them or remember from childhood, join new religions and new sects and, from Bahai to Pentecostalism, every religion builds.

The Functions of Buildings in the Development of Religion

A religious building is far more than a place to visit or meet in. It speaks out its meaning to the world and it embodies – shaped as it is by people, living and dead, and their practices – the quintessence of a religious tradition, old or new. It is nonsense to say that buildings do not matter. Why are the early manifestations of outbreaks of antisemitism almost always attacks on synagogues, if not because the synagogue *represents* the Jewish community? Why does any government repressive of religion or a particular form of it, so often demand that religious buildings should be stripped of anything that identifies them, deprived of access to a road, removed from a street map, if not because the building is the public face of a religious community by which it may be known?

The power exerted by buildings and even by sites accounts for the persistence with which new religions build on top of what they want to change, supplant or destroy. Many different attitudes of religions to other religions are expressed in these actions. Muslims frequently took over Christian churches: they removed all Christian symbols, adapted the interior for their own religious use, added minarets and reoriented the building towards Mecca. Christianity, they were saying, had betrayed the cause of absolute monotheism and lost simplicity of worship: these Mohammed renewed. Like him, they were correcting error. Christians built over temples of Mithras or incorporated parts of them into new buildings: Mithras was superseded. The religion of the Aztecs of Mexico was a different matter. The site used by the Aztecs for human sacrifices in the middle of the city was totally destroyed and over it a vast cathedral was built. Even allowing for the un-canny effects of earthquakes in creating the undulating floor and the cracked pillars and walls, the hugeness of the building still conveys the impression of a frantic effort to leave nothing outside its obliterating purposes.

Probably a good deal of what is said about the 'atmosphere' of religious buildings is the sentimental nonsense that realists say it is. A whiff of incense, some stained glass, candlelight and semi-darkness make some people 'feel religious' or sense the aura of holiness of bygone users. Ruins affect people with the sadness and the relief of feeling that what was is no more. But yielding to such amorphous feelings as 'atmosphere' can stand in the way of a far more satisfying appreciation.

Non-believers are inclined to say that they can appreciate a great religious building 'as art' but not 'as religion'. Will such a contention hold? These buildings were built and adorned by men for the use of people: people who found or find in the action and symbolism of worship some clue to the problem of human destiny, some means of preserving human significance against the terrifying possibilities of life and of death, some expression of human community and some restraint against its destruction. The architects, builders and craftsmen are using the language of their work to convey something of the purpose and vision that inspired a building, for they were part of what it has to say. The link between them and us is not art or religion but humanity. Even if we have rejected religious faith, if we really 'hear' the language of a great religious building it is telling us something about *ourselves*. Because as humans we came that way, something of us is already there in what we see.

It is an odd reflection that, although the men of the Middle Ages or the contemporaries of Mohammed are no more than a minute or a mile away from us on any evolutionary scale of time and place, yet we feel that we have more to learn from, and that it would be easier to understand, the behaviour of animals than the religious behaviour of other men. *The Times* made a little stir by suggesting in its Christmas leader in 1967 that if the peace and goodwill of which Christmas speaks are ever to become realities men will need to learn from the sociologist and the student of animal behaviour. Why not? Any light on our problems is surely welcome. But is it not possible that the study of what men actually do in religion and what makes men religious, and religious in different ways, is quite as relevant as the study of the ritualized aggression of sticklebacks? Religion, like war, acts out what lies within. But have we minds accessible to this knowledge or are we too blinkered, by rejection of all religion or pre-occupation with the subjectivity of our own, to see religion as a revealer of the human heart and building as one of its languages?

If buildings express the essence of a religion they do so not only through individual works of genius but through the creation of a style. Within a particular style lesser men make a contribution which is less than a work of genius but more than an imitation. This style is as closely related to the heart of a particular religion as domestic architecture is to a way of life in a given climate. The minaret, in origin and name a beacon, is not only a practical way of calling the faithful to prayer: it symbolizes the calling of Islam to constant vigilance. The spire embodies the aspiration that its name implies. The towers of Buddhist temples, often bubble-shaped and reflecting back the light that falls on them, wordlessly express the secondary and transitory nature of this world.

Most religious buildings of any considerable age have been added to or adapted. Sometimes we deplore the result, while we scarcely notice additions and changes so skilfully made that they blend into a new whole. Part of this is due to the skill of architects or builders, but the power of a tradition to develop the appropriate visual expression of changing ideas underlies the skills. The perfection of the Taj Mahal is that of a tomb: nothing more needs to be said. A religious building still in use changes subtly all the time. The fear that religious buildings would ossify as 'ancient monuments' lies behind the refusal of many religious bodies to hand over the control of their buildings to the state. There are often arguments when the claims of preservation and of use do not coincide. The question 'whose buildings are they?' is not one that can be answered in a sentence or generalized about. Lack of use or lack of funds to keep it in repair may turn a building into a monument or a ruin and when that point has been reached religious bodies have to decide whether to invite some other body, usually the state, to assume responsibility. All over the world states, even the anti-religious, are concerned about the preservation of religious buildings which almost always form one of the largest portions of the antiquities of a nation. Many have been rescued from oblivion only by state action. On the other hand there are exceptions: the Albanian communist government has now completed the process of razing to the ground every religious building, church or mosque, but posters still warn the public to protect children against the dangers of religion.

Shrine and Meeting Place

The enormous growth of tourism encourages the growth of an attitude towards religious buildings which looks at them only in terms of the past. A Punch cartoon shows a group of tourists climbing out of their bus at the steps of St. Paul's Cathedral. 'Oh dear', says the courier, 'we've come at the wrong time: there's a service going on'. A German school-teacher was overheard saying to her charges on a visit to Bristol 'now children, today we shall be visiting some of the churches in the city because they are the monuments of our dead past'. She was standing at the time in a church college of education with something of a reputation for contemporary worship.

An exactly opposite point of view is to look at religious buildings as a total stock of buildings for use in the present. In spite of great differences of age, size and condition, they constitute what is available for the uses of religion.

They are of two main kinds: some are wholly or mainly *shrines*, others are wholly or mainly regular *meeting-places* for corporate acts.

The religious buildings of Hinduism, and of Buddhism except for monasteries for resident communities, are almost entirely shrines. They are visited by individuals or parties of people who make their own offerings and devotions with or without the help of priest or monk. Shrines usually grow up over some relic, associated with a great teacher or a holy man or with some event, miraculous or not (the place where Dr. Ambedkar, Indian outcaste leader, embraced Buddhism is now a shrine). Associated with most larger shrines are festivals – times for the celebration of great events common to thousands of shrines and times for the celebration of the local event, person or god to which the shrine is particularly dedicated. While some shrines retain their popularity over long periods, other become suddenly famous and popular and then fall into neglect. They may be famous for healing, or for prayer for particular needs, or for the merit that accrues from visiting them, or for the interest of visiting the burial place of some famous person. Shrines invite pilgrimages, a type of religious exercise common to many religions. The point about a shrine is that it is *visited*, not *attended*: nobody except the priests or monks who may care for it can be said to *belong* to it.

Of quite a different character is the religious building that is the home of a regular congregation or stands in a unique relationship to a local community, as does a parish church. Such buildings as these are arranged to receive people in companies at stated times for corporate worship or other corporate acts. A synagogue is this sort of religious building, so is a mosque, so is a Christian church. Several common factors help to make them so – the existence in Judaism, Islam and Christianity of one day of the week marked out for special prayer, the insistence of each on the corporate nature of religion, the habit of reading and expounding scriptures publicly. Christian churches can be both shrines and the homes of a regular community, as one can see in many Roman Catholic churches where the habit of occasional visiting and personal devotion at an altar or before some sacred object goes on in the same building as corporate attendance at mass. To many Christians, however, the idea of a church as a shrine has something offensive about it, smacking of idolatry and superstition at worst and individualism at best. One may however ask whether the habit of calling so many Methodist churches 'Wesley Memorial' and many Baptist and Congregational churches after revered leaders – 'Parker Memorial', 'Hall Memorial' – is not an unconscious survival of the shrine aspect of religious buildings.

Europe was Christianized mainly from large bases where the missionaries from elsewhere settled and built a minster or abbey. In the extremely unsettled times of the early missionary expansion these centres often acted as retreats and defences and they were the target for marauders. In England not a single one of the Celtic or Anglo-Saxon abbeys escaped looting and fire at the hands of the Danes. The building of parish churches was a slow process, only possible as conditions grew more settled. Most British and European parish churches date from the Middle Ages or later. Mass was the only regular service and it is difficult to tell how many people went regularly: certainly there were many parishes ill-provided with priests to say it regularly, what with absentees, livings held in plurality and other deviations. There were no seats, except along the wall, to which the weakest went. Parts of the building and especially the nave and the porch were used for other purposes than religious ones. It was a place, almost always the *only* place for people to gather under cover. How did it become a place that some people attend on Sundays?

The forerunners of the '11 a.m. and 6.30 p.m.' services on a Sunday, common to the Church of England and the Free Churches, at least as to times and length, only came into church life in England in Tudor times. They were provided as public worship in parish churches in the first Book of Common Prayer in 1549. What quirk of conscience perhaps prompted the authorities to compensate for ending the regular saying of offices in the monasteries by fastening on the clergy and laity, by Act of Parliament, services which were mainly compounded out of rearrangements of monastic offices? Thus it has come about that today the yardstick of 'belonging' used by census takers or polesters or the general public is attendance at *these* services which the Church for centuries got on without.

Another factor to change the internal organization and use of church buildings was the Reformers' emphasis on the authority and therefore exposition of the Bible. Preaching, and therefore pulpits, became more prominent. People spent a large part of the time at the new services in listening. But the Reformers favoured singing: first the psalms and later, but gradually, new hymns came into worship. Curiously enough, the less churches looked like places of worship with the progressive removal of pictures, images, stained glass, candles, tabernacles, fonts and all the traditional aids to worship, the more exclusively were they used for worship and worship alone. While a church was mainly or partly a shrine people gossiped around in it and all the aids to devotion were provided for them. But the sitting congregations began to bring in their own aids – Sunday clothes and Sunday faces, Bibles and prayer books, and they rented and reserved seats and furnished them with comfort. These things drew new distinctions between better-off and poor, literate and illiterate, belonger and casuals. The sense of having no place in a church which was once 'everybody's place' is still keenly felt, however many welcoming notices flutter in the porch.

Anglican and Lutheran reformers made the least changes in existing buildings. Lutherans made more of the pulpit, Anglicans moved the altar to the east end of the church and made provision for the audible reading of the Bible. Some early accounts say that when it was first read in English people crowded to the front to hear. Roman Catholics do not usually feel that Anglicans and Lutherans have 'ruined' the buildings they once possessed. All three went on building in the same tradition while they hurled abuse at one another. But the Reformed (presbyterian) tradition was far more radical. In Holland, for example, it is not uncommon to see old churches whose interior arrangement has been turned back to front, with the congregation facing westwards, the altar removed, the chancel forlornly used as a store for extra chairs and rolls of carpet or a place for wedding receptions.

The violent reaction of Roman Catholic authority to the Reformation and the disagreements between the Reformers led to wars and civil strife and broke up the tottering unity of Christendom. But most Reformers were no more minded than the Pope himself that ordinary people in towns and villages should have a *choice* of different types of worship provided under a variety of auspices in a variety of buildings. They were as eager for unity, even uniformity, as any medievalist. The growth of national selfconsciousness in many parts of Europe helped to make a unity of religion on a new basis within the newly-forming state boundaries, or under the acknowledged secular leadership of an area. Within that area deviations were frowned upon. The Reformers used every device they knew to make reform lasting, meaningful and unified. Calvin's *Institutes of Religion*, Luther's German Bible and his catechism, Cranmer's prayer book, all had these ends in view. That the state should endorse and support these ends seemed to them right. For the state of course it was stability and unity that were the most important.

Minority bodies, groups of men and women who felt that the Reformers had not gone far enough in their reforms and who protested against the new alliances of church and state that made religion into a test of political loyalty, emerged quickly in the wake of reform. Many of them were convinced that adult baptism was the only proper form of the rite of entry into the church; all laid stress on the local community of believers, not in the sense of being the local population gathered together but as a group from among the population, held together by common bonds of faith and practice, regulated by the Bible as their supreme authority. As a persecuted or unprivileged minority they could not build: they met in houses and (if Baptists) baptized in rivers. But when they gained toleration they built in a new style of religious building, to be seen in early Quaker meeting houses and the late seventeenth-century chapels of Baptists and Congregationalists. These groups had different origins and varied principles but they shared a common style of building, which is not, and cannot be, a shrine. Its shape is a room, oblong or square. The pulpit or the desk for the clerk may be in the middle of the long side and the seats are (or were until moved) often on three sides facing inwards. The simplicity of these early buildings with their little graveyards perfectly reflects the principles of those who built them: in life and in death they were to be a *community* separated out from among the population, bound together by a covenant with God and one another in the belief that (as one of the early leaders said) 'the kingdom of God is begun not by whole parishes but by the most worthy, be they never so few'. The revival of the Greek classical style in the eighteenth century well suited the growing affluence of some of these groups while keeping to the room-like form of the interior with tall windows unadorned by coloured glass. Such buildings can be found today in the main streets of many country towns.

Methodism, emerging as a separate church from the Church of England only at the very end of the eighteenth century, reached its most active period of building after the Industrial Revolution, in the period of red brick. As they multiplied methodists built, and as they split and re-split, they built and built again so that some towns and even villages had chapels at each end. In the big industrial towns where the crowds gathered to hear popular preachers, large structures, sometimes with galleries supported on iron pillars and en-closed with iron railings, were provided: they can only have been tolerable when they rang to the singing of hymns. But the hearts of the great cities were a challenge to all denomina-tions and though they built churches few were filled with the poor among whom they were hopefully to be a sobering and uplifting influence. What could be done by buildings reached the end of its possibilities and William Booth and his Salvationists took to the streets and alleys of the slums and used empty shops as their bases.

Schools and Church Premises

At the time of the 1944 Education Act nearly two-thirds of England's schools were church schools. They contained a little over one-third of the country's children. A few were old grammar schools, some were the charity schools of the eighteenth century. The great majority of schools were the 'National' and 'British' Schools built in the nineteenth century by Church of England and nonconformist societies founded in 1811 and 1809 respectively.[1] After 1840 they also began to erect training colleges for teachers. The nonconformists abandoned school building almost entirely after the middle of the century, but the Church of England and the Roman Catholics (who began building schools rather later when Irish immigration began)[2] went ahead with every intention of staving off state control. Few things did the Church of England more harm in the first half of the twentieth century than the wretched condition of many of its school buildings and few free churchmen look back with any pride on the ferocity with which their forebears tried to prevent aid from the state for the luckless children in these fortresses. Following the 1944 Act the Church of England let more than half its nearly 8,000 schools go 'controlled' and began to put the remaining ones in order and to build new ones. Since 1960 it has enlarged all its colleges of education and built two new ones. There are now over 2,000 Roman Catholic, over 3,000 Church of England, and a small number of Methodist and other denominational schools in church ownership as

[1] For the history of the national schools see H. BURGESS, *Enterprise in Education* (S.P.C.K., 1958) and M. CRUIKSHANK, *Church and State in English Education* (Macmillan, 1963).

[2] See H. O. EVENNETT, *The Catholic Schools of England and Wales* (Oxford, 1944) and J. W. ADAMSON, *History of Education in England 1792–1902* (Cambridge, 1930).

'aided' schools.[1] The Roman Catholic Church kept all its schools as 'aided' schools, has added to their size and number at a cost of £100 million in twenty years and has a large building programme involving a heavy financial commitment of £4 million per annum for the dioceses and parishes.

*

By 1800 about 600,000 children and adults were receiving religious instruction and learning to read and write in Sunday Schools. These activities and others like the class meetings of Methodism had to be housed, and thus began the new and most characteristic feature of nineteenth-century church-building, the complex of buildings containing halls, class-rooms, committee rooms, kitchens, common rooms, providing space for a growing range of activities broadening out from the specifically religious to the more general social and educational, and providing for many age and interest groups. Many more people used these buildings than regularly attended the worship of the church or chapel. Roman Catholic parishes developed in a rather different way. Most of them were poor and were composed of families with little or no leisure. Every parish had its school but few had the money or the need to build anything else.

*

In the United States early church building used the materials that were to hand, notably wood. The colonial style of building in the New England colonies lent itself to combining the room-shaped interior of the puritans with the graceful spire that marked it as being, in a country without parish churches, the nearest equivalent – once more the church of a local population. But some of the older denominations were slower to respond to the needs of populations moving west-

[1] The terms 'aided' and 'controlled' were devised for the 1944 Act: the former gives the trustees a larger share of control and more financial obligation than the latter.

wards into rough country than the later comers, Methodists, Baptists and new, specifically American, bodies. The constitutional separation of church and state gave no privilege to any one denomination but the possibility of equal development to all, therefore those who went with the frontier as it moved west gained the pre-eminence in the areas where they settled. American church buildings in some areas still reflect the pattern of early settlement of national groups from every part of Europe. But no matter what their European background, the buildings are shaped both by worship and by their function as the rallying point of whole communities for many of their cultural and leisure needs. No wonder that William Whyte's book *The Organization Man* has a chapter on the churches, devoted to the men who are the managers of such plants, the clergy and the full-time lay employees of the churches.

Outside the Anglo-Saxon world a different style of church architecture has been developed from a tradition untouched by protestantism, that of colonial Spain and Portugal. Central and South America portray not only the baroque grandeur of cathedrals, but the austere simplicity of small churches built by the religious orders. In this century Brazil, where the Portuguese domestic style has developed with a peculiar felicity of adaptation, architecture is the supreme national art. In Brazil and in Argentina the churches have adopted modern architectural styles. The fastest growing of them, the Pentecostal churches, have some spectacular modern buildings – and they are packed with people of all classes.

Christianity is more heavily endowed with buildings than any other religion. One must allow in making this judgement for the physical climate of the northern hemisphere, the main area of Christianity: but even so, its primary urge is to gather people together. It has always assumed that the form of the church was the local community. But the future raises question marks against that supposition.

III

BUILDINGS: PRESENT INTO FUTURE

In a society characterized by mobility buildings are the most static part of religion. All over the world ruins and deserted buildings point to a former presence and departure of populations, the rise and fall of empires, the exhaustion of the soil, the end of a colonial exploit, the closure of a coal pit. Great mounds cover ancient temples. This has been going on for all recorded history and longer, but never has there been so large-scale and world-wide a movement of populations as in our own day or so continuous a single trend. The great majority of all these migrants are going to the cities.

Household gods and little shrines are portable and go with the religious-minded. The Buddhist can make his shrine in his room. The Muslim takes his prayer mat. If they lose their religion it is less likely to be from lack of a building than from the changes of the rhythm of life between country and city. A man is no longer near to nature: or the hours fixed for his work by the bus corporation interfere with the hours of prayer. Shrines appear in city streets: religious pictures adorn shops and are garlanded. There is plenty of commercial exploitation of superstition: charms and horoscopes abound, but without some community to sustain them the moral sanctions of religion are under strain in new circumstances, and prayer and devotion fall into disuse.

Christianity like Judaism has always been a religion of community which demanded for its performance that people should gather together for worship and for some sort of common life. It was preached in rural Galilee, but the church

began in Jerusalem and spread along the trade routes of the
Roman world from one city to another. Its members were
often emigrants or even migrants – craftsmen, slaves, shop-
keepers and merchants: not a people dependent directly on
the land. Their modern counterparts in the cities of today
are often the Christian sects. Japan has myriads of them,
fulfilling in some way the needs of uprooted people and
urban masses by providing a community and a dimension
beyond the round of work and the physical world. It is not
surprising that Buddhism has developed a form of parish life
in industrial Japan.

For centuries the community life of Christianity has been
associated with buildings, even expressed through them. A
considerable debate is now going on about whether this
connection is necessary, whether it can go on and whether it
should. Some Christians are saying that after centuries of a
'come' structure, that is of churches inviting men into their
buildings, organized religion as far as Christianity is concerned must develop a 'go' structure, that is disperse its active
members into society to make personal contact in small
groups and to take their share in secular organizations of
work, leisure and service. It is argued that money is spent on
buildings that could be better spent in other ways. Those who
have to live that way under suppression show what can
be done; the faith can continue in families and the life of
Christians be lived largely *incognito* in the world.

Salutary as such challenges are, it is not easy to see that
they could become the active principles for the conduct of
Christianity, given its nature as a community religion. For it
is a community religion not only in the sense of gathering
isolated communities: those single communities are connected at however distant a range with a world-wide inter-
communication of communities engaged in worship and
community activity of many kinds. Mr. Malcolm Mugger-

idge describes how he walks across the Sussex fields to a country church where he joins a few old ladies at the service and calculates that perhaps it will last his time. However, he might perhaps meditate on the strange paradox that these and other local congregations together form 'a major source of private development assistance to the developing nations with a significantly larger service budget than most of the United Nations development agencies combined'.[1] Mr. David Martin in an article entitled 'A sociologist among the theologians'[2] says that those who talk critically of the amount the churches spend on maintaining their organization and buildings would, if they made comparisons, find that the cost of maintaining *any* base for action, whether in education or social service, is no less.

If then the radical solution of de-organization is not a positive option for the Christian religion, what ought to be done? In relation to buildings what are the problems that the past has set to the present and the future for their solution?

Problems from the Past

The first problem is the sheer numerical superfluity of buildings and the fact that many of them are in the wrong places. England is more afflicted in this way than either the continent of Europe or the United States: the history outlined in the last chapter shows why. 'Empty churches' is one of the commonest ways of describing the decline of religion: the existence of too many buildings accelerates decline because of

[1] Quoted from a report written by Dr. Richard Dickinson for the World Council of Churches and published by them in August, 1968. Dr. Dickinson has surveyed church institutions in India and elsewhere for the Dutch Foundation ISS–FERES and for the Ford Foundation, U.S.A. His latest report contains the best (and best written) account of the problems of development and the churches' present and future role.

[2] *The Listener*, 25 April 1968.

the depressing effect and the financial burden on a small congregation. Russia has no empty churches, except those that have been forcibly closed: on the contrary they are packed to suffocation. In proportion to total population, England has twice as many churches as the United States, but since some sixty per cent of Americans are affiliated to a church – a far higher proportion than in England – the actual disparity in this country between needs and provision is even greater. But which buildings should go? Some of the churches' previous abandonments have been mistakes – even disasters. Following the prospering congregation out from the city centre to the new suburb and leaving the new poor unprovided is an example of how not to abandon buildings.[1] A newly awakened ecumenical conscience makes it impossible to insist that all the buildings of all the denominations are needed or could be supported in the future. With their joint resources and an informed eye on development plans and with good co-operation with civic authorities, mistakes of the past need not be repeated.

Secondly there is the problem of who the church building is for. Many parish churches have become, like free churches, the home of a gathered congregation collecting together from inside and outside the geographical parish. But the parish priest is incumbent of a living: his parish is the people of a geographical area, not the congregation alone, and much of his service is given to non-attenders. The congregation needs a building: what does the parish need?

Thirdly, what sort of buildings are needed if Christians are to achieve the aim they are now seeing with increasing clarity: that the church building is a means to an end and must not be an end in itself? How can they create or adapt buildings that will enable them to worship with greater

---

[1] Examples of this in Sheffield are described by E. R. WICKHAM, *Church and People in an Industrial City* (Lutterworth Press, 1957).

reality and serve their neighbours beyond their institutions, with greater effectiveness?

Three Categories of Buildings for the Future

The Shrine. Buildings for future needs might be considered in three categories. First, the future of the shrine, the building that is visited rather than attended, whose congregation, if it has one, needs to be committed to the service that such buildings can uniquely render. These buildings are the cathedrals and the large churches (not necessarily of the establishment) in big towns and cities.

In most countries of Europe great and ancient cathedrals are maintained from state funds: their fabric and treasures are cared for by experts; no alarmed appeals have to be made for money to prevent the tower or the roof from collapse. Many think that the same situation will have to be reached in England, but many more disagree and are to some extent supported in their view by the fact that appeals for cathedrals do not fail. The labour of appealing is heavy, but it is not in vain. The money comes from industries, local authorities, public bodies, trusts, private individuals, church organizations and from the parishes of the diocese. Yorkshire being ecclesiastically five dioceses has no less than five cathedrals, yet York Minster appealing in 1967 for two million pounds was well on the way to getting it a year later. Local pride everywhere, which is steadily deprived of rallying points, would regard it as a humiliating thing to have 'our cathedral' taken over by Whitehall. Most cathedrals, often with the support of 'Friends' of the cathedral make great efforts to get the cathedral known, valued and used, and to make the use modern and diverse. Cathedrals were built for the glory of God, as places where worship would be offered and also as places that would themselves be an offering of beauty. Becoming accustomed to ugliness in our environment and tolerating what is hideous or lifelessly dull is to put the human spirit into a kind of prison. Both Christianity and Islam have built with exquisite grace and formidable strength. The care and use of what we inherit is not only a responsibility to the future but a challenge to it to have the singleness of heart from which beauty springs and to ponder the relationship there once was between the pursuit of immaterial ends and the power over material means. Many of the beauties of cathedrals are seen better now by modern flood-lighting and television cameras than they have been since the workmen took the last scaffolding away centuries ago. To be beautiful and to engender the love of God as the source of beauty is part of their vocation. They impart to other lovely things far more than mere 'background': they become part of an act of worship and for many modern people music and drama performed in them convey not only what Bach or Elgar or Britten intended but something of the meaning of worship which they often do not find in services.

The re-building of Coventry Cathedral has been one of the great events in English religious life in the past twenty years.[1] It had also a national significance. The destruction of the old cathedral and the creation of the new have been a national parable of death and life. The church was felt to be doing something *new*, building in an old tradition, but in the modern mood. And the cathedral authorities took the sight-seeing and the tours in their stride and went out to meet people with more of the common touch than is often displayed. A youth centre and an international centre on the site (the latter mainly the work of German young people), are a practical expression of Christianity in the modern world used by young people from all over the country and beyond. The cathedral has also gone out to the industry of the city,

[1] STEPHEN VERNEY, *Fire in Coventry* (Hodder & Stoughton, 1964), describes the working out of plans for the use of the new cathedral.

trying through its chapel of industry and the work of industrial chaplaincy to make a bridge between religion and modern daily life. Coventry cathedral is a modern interpretation of the idea of shrine and of pilgrimage, not to the bones of a saint but to a modern symbol of action in the world, in which the ruins of the old cathedral, open to the sky and used for drama and worship, play a significant part.

A substantial part of the cost of re-building Coventry Cathedral came from government compensation for war damage. Undertakings on such a scale are probably now out of reach of the churches and outside their present priorities. A more modest effort, with many of the same aims and effects, has been the rebuilding of the abbey on the island of Iona. This began with the founding of the Iona Community, a body of young Church of Scotland ministers based on two community houses in the poorer parts of Edinburgh and Glasgow and working in parishes in these and other cities. In the course of many summers they and some of the lay associates of the community worked under the skilled direction of stone masons to restore the abbey church and add other buildings. This is complete and has become both a continuous place of pilgrimage as the birthplace of Christianity in Scotland, and a training centre for young people from many churches all over the world. Many examples could be given from Europe of a return to traditional sites to rebuild, for modern needs, places for retreat, worship and training.

Westminster Abbey and St. George's Chapel, Windsor, are both *national* shrines with a strong appeal to Commonwealth and American visitors. Neither rests content with the role of museum and showplace: the one keeps to a strong tradition of preaching especially on social and international issues and has also sponsored a new and very successful venture of small groups exploring for faith: the other has created a residential centre within the buildings attached to the chapel where similar kinds of exploration can be undertaken.

The Meeting Place. The second type of church building is the local church for a regular congregation and the use of the people in a parish or an area.

For at least a hundred years – roughly from the forties of last century to the second world war – a very large influence both in church and in national life was wielded in the Protestant countries of Europe, in Britain and North America by the great churches of cities. Their main strength was in the preaching which drew large congregations of mainly educated and often influential people. From these pulpits the voice of the nonconformist conscience was heard in England, the volleys of theological debate were loosed in Scotland, the evangelical warmed his hearers' hearts or the intellectual divine tackled some of the mind-stretching problems posed to the Christian faith by the scientific developments of the nineteenth century.

In a small study of several Edinburgh churches called *Journey to Church* Sir George McLeod, leader of the Iona Community, showed the high proportion of the congregations of these churches who made the journey in from the suburbs. Long before the Rev. Nicholas Stacey was telling readers of *The Observer* how impossible it was to do anything with Woolwich parish church in relation to the local residents, that church had ceased to be a local church and its congregations were coming from a distance to hear such well-known preachers as its rector, the present bishop of Coventry. The mass media, the decline of preaching as a medium of political protest or theological debate (a decline accompanied by a great rise in the number and circulation of books on the same themes), the rise of fares and many other factors have helped to bring about a diminution of the role of city churches as congregations. Another factor is the growth of churches in outer suburbia, now containing examples of the strongest part of local church-life and much dead wood also.

Some city churches turned to a different and specialized function. St. Martins in the Fields, London, became the prototype of churches offering a ministry to people in desperate need. Its annual radio appeal is still one of the most generously supported of all such appeals. Churches in provincial cities perform a similar role and one can parallel it with the work of German parishes for refugees and of Parisian parishes for the destitute, of East Harlem, New York, among the negro and Puerto Rican poor. Some have turned to new needs. In London, St. Bride's, Fleet Street, has become the church of the press, the Samaritans started from St. Stephen's, Walbrook, St. Paul's, Lancaster Gate, set out to meet the needs of young people living in the waste-land of bed-sitters that surrounds the church; the bombed Methodist mission in the Lambeth Road has used part of its land to build a hostel for overseas students and a club for the many who live in the area, trying to make a contribution to good race relations there.

Many national groups belonging to continental denominations have the use of redundant city churches in many parts of the world where services and pastoral help are available in the language of the few regulars and the many migrants and travellers who make use of them. Church buildings have also been made over in some cases to immigrants of non-Christian faith. These are only a few of the many examples of a new, much less spectacular use of old buildings that could be given, and of the gathering together of people along other lines than those of the traditional, resident and largely stationary local congregation. Such needs are not likely to diminish.

The French Catholics were the first to use social studies to trace evolving social patterns and so to throw light on where to build churches, what was needed, where money and men could be concentrated with the greatest effectiveness. The Dutch, again especially the Catholics, were not far behind them: they explored the possibilities of Catholics and Protestants using the same buildings at different times: this was also found to be possible in Austria. Gone are the days when large housing estates were erected without a shop, a pub or a church, or when the church waited for the new inhabitants to arrive before any action was taken. A number of dioceses in England now have planning officers whose business it is to study plans for development and to work with local authorities on the question of sites, and types of building. The need to re-build after the war brought the churches together in the first instance for the assessment of war damage and later to plan new building jointly. In many new housing estates and in new towns the curate or the young minister, and the woman worker, are among the first to arrive, their initial task being to help people with the problems of change and to join in creating a community out of separate families uprooted and unknown to one another.

Between 1945 and 1965 the Church of England erected over 1,000 new churches, halls and dual-purpose buildings, costing £17 million, and its dioceses are planning to erect a further 1,100 buildings in the decade from 1965 to 1975. £13 million will be spent in the first five years and the total cost is estimated at not less than £20 million. Nearly all this building is in areas of new settlement. Roman Catholic spending on new churches is between £1½ and £2 million per annum and Methodists, the largest of the Free Churches, are also as deeply committed financially to their church-extension programmes.

The churches are not building in competition with one another: joint planning is common and shared use will become commoner in the future. There are sixteen church-sharing schemes in operation, forty under consideration, (many in new towns) and nineteen joint Anglican–Methodist schemes, with every likelihood that this number will leap up if the first stage of Anglican–Methodist union comes into action soon. Congregationalists and Presbyterians are already combining locally in anticipation of the union of the two churches in 1970. The Church of England is prevented by law from sharing the ownership of a church building with other churches but the possibility of an Act of Parliament to permit this freedom is being explored. Joint 'pastoral centres' have been built, or are being planned, for new towns, and some thirty youth centres.

In all this the people who will use the buildings are having an increasing share of the planning of them, working jointly with architects. New materials make far more flexible designs possible, including the temporary building that can be taken down and moved elsewhere. Existing congregations are the main financial supporters and often supply personal help in the early stages of growth: but the dioceses with the help of advisors such as the Central Council for the Care of Churches are the initiators and planners.

New church buildings are designed round developments in worship not vice versa. The possibility of further unforeseen developments is always in mind. The long narrow church designed for a mainly receptive, largely non-participating congregation is giving way to the more nearly square, circular or octagonal building. Furniture tends to be simple and moveable to give choice in use. Many artists and designers are commissioned for special work and the traditional partnership between the church and the arts is thus being carried on.

New buildings are also being built in universities and colleges. Hull, Keele and Sussex have, and Lancaster will have, new chapels for shared use – all very unlike the college chapels of Oxford and Cambridge with their long rows of inward-facing pews.

Colleges of education as they have expanded have turned their Victorian chapels into libraries and built modern ones. The debate about a chapel that takes place on many university campuses and is decided in many different ways is a theological education in itself. For not only is there vociferous opposition to religious buildings in secular universities from the side of those who are not believers but the believers themselves are divided on the advantages and disadvantages of having set-apart buildings for wholly or mainly religious purposes. On the whole this opposition to 'special religious buildings' is gaining ground. On many university sites there is regular worship on Sundays in lecture-rooms, common-rooms, labs and even the union bar, and those who feel something of the foot-looseness of pioneers often have little desire to acquire a building,[1] while others prefer to make their contacts with local churches or to use the period of university as the time to remove oneself from religious commitment.

But new building is not the only or even the main way of providing for local needs. Many old buildings overtaken by influxes of population have been enlarged and restructured. Again, this is done as part of diocesan or central planning and by architects. Many who look at the rather forbidding exteriors of church buildings might find a high proportion of them surprisingly well cared for inside. There is more money to spend, indeed commercial firms find it worth their while to organize exhibitions of church furnishings and furniture because so much is spent. But an increasingly tender con-

[1] I have noticed in the programme of a community centre in a new town that the only two religious bodies to advertise meetings within the centre are those without their own buildings in the town – Mormons and Jehovah's Witnesses.

science irks some individuals and congregations: what about the needs of churches in poor districts, in areas of racial tension, or overseas, where there is far more to do and much less of resources of any kind. It is right to adorn buildings for the worship of God and reasonable to keep them in good order and make them pleasant places: but when do these desirable ends shade off into satisfying the comfort and the corporate possessiveness of the worshippers?

Using Buildings for Communication

Another point of discussion about the future of religion is how religious buildings can be used to make a means of communication with those outside the faith for whose practice they have been built. A great many religious buildings are not available for use by others than the faithful. Most religions make distinctions between men and women and either exclude women from the whole building or reserve a gallery or other place where they can see but not take part. While the building as a whole seen from the outside is a witness to the faith, the inside is for the faithful and not for communicating with the unbeliever. The Christian church relies very little now on what goes on inside churches to bring the meaning and claims of religion to those outside them. Nor does it rely on taking the methods used in the church into the street. Homes have become a place of communication, hence 'the house church', 'the living-room dialogue', the neighbourhood group. The communication of the Christian faith goes on mainly by informal means. If an evangelist wants to try to communicate the faith to large numbers of people he and his organizers hire a stadium, not St. Paul's Cathedral. Perhaps the time will come again when inquirers go into churches to find out about Christianity: not many do so now.

Can the church premises that the congregation uses for a

very small part of the week and only for those additional activities that its members have the time and enthusiasm to organize be used for meeting other needs in the local community? That old but serviceable hall next to the bus stop may be exactly the right place for the citizen's advice bureau or the foot clinic for old people, or the play group for the children who can no longer be safely allowed to play on the street or the group of Indian women needing to be taught English or the extra class at the tech., for which there is no room. These are a few growingly typical examples and are due to a greater willingness of churches to let or lend their premises and of local authorities not to grudge a few night-storage heaters and a small rent if it can get accommodation it cannot find. Unwillingness to take part in what it could not run has been an unfortunate characteristic of much church activity in the past: now the advantages of allowing someone else to do the organizing and pay skilled help where it is needed, are being gradually realized. The willing amateur can then find a proper and more effective place, and the church discovers that it has more links with the community and opportunities to serve, using its buildings in new ways.

'Evangelical Academies' are by now a well-known experiment in communication between the church and the community of a particular industrial or farming area. The largest of them, very handsomely housed with residential accommodation, libraries, common rooms and lecture rooms and staffed with economists, sociologists, theologians and appropriate administration, are in Germany where the existence of the church tax has made the finances of such large projects less daunting. But under the same or more felicitous names there are similar new institutions in Scandinavia, France, Holland, Switzerland, the United States and Great Britain. Although they usually serve a region many encourage international contacts. Largely on German initiative and through the World Council of Churches aid has been forthcoming for similar projects in developing countries. Some of these institutions, by studying the problems of an area – social, economic and industrial – and by then providing the sort of venue where religious problems can be discussed freely (on an inter-faith basis sometimes) have met with real success in that they get people thinking about vital community problems. More conservative church-goers comment that such efforts even if they touch many outsiders do not fill the pews, but that is not their object. There is room only for a few examples of new types of buildings erected by churches and by Christian voluntary organizations. Lay organizations such as the Y.M.C.A. and Y.W.C.A. have recently undertaken large programmes for hostels for apprentices and flats for business girls. Other organizations concentrate on homes for children, for unmarried mothers and their babies, for delinquents, for ex-prisoners, for the old. New holiday camps and hostels for migrant workers, international houses for overseas students and housing associations for the purchase and reconditioning of property for families in desperate need are examples of post-war initiatives of the churches themselves. Many others could be cited.

If the ability to re-develop resources on new building and to attract new income for such projects and their running costs are signs of institutional flexibility, then the institutions of religion still have more initiative than many think. But is eagerness to build matched by an equal power to adapt and initiate in other spheres?

IV

THE PROFESSIONALS: JEWISH; HINDU; BUDDHIST

EVERY religion has its special persons set apart for particular religious duties. The history of religions shows how these élites persist, constantly reforming after periods of persecution or disruption, changing with social circumstances, adapting to foreign situations, reappearing in a recognizable continuity of function and office in new or break-away sects. Most religions have more than one type of person recognized as in some sense 'special' and it is quite false to religion in all its vastness and variety to assume that every religion has *one* élite which can simply be called the priesthood. Religions (but not all religions) have persons set apart for making sacrifices or offering worship, and 'one who performs these functions' would be the commonest definition of a priest. But in every religion there are many other élites, formal and informal. They include monks and nuns, holy men, scholars and teachers, prophets, healers, missionaries and many others some of whom may also be priests. For the future of religion this diversification may be of considerable importance.

But in spite of the diversity of élites there is always one élite in any religion that constitutes its main authority. It may not be authority to accept or reject persons as adherents, or to govern by rewards and sanctions the life they lead. But it will be at a minimum the authority to perform the most important rites and to say what *goes* in the religious tradition; at the maximum it will be far more. Everybody knows that there is now a crisis of authority in religion. Whereas past crises have mainly been about who should hold authority, the present one is about the nature of religious authority as such. This immediately broadens the question from what persons hold authority and what authority they hold to other questions such as the authority of religious institutions in relation to other institutions in society (a question very different today from the question of church and state in its historical context), the authority of religious knowledge and teaching, measured against other knowledge.

No didactic statement is more out of fashion today than 'History teaches us that. . . .' There are areas of life in which one can say that history teaches very little and even that reference to the past is at best a distraction and may be a hindrance. The professional élites of religion are caught between two fires. There is a certain readiness for change: in some quarters a very strong appeal for change even among those most effectively placed to carry it out, namely the leaders. But in every religion leaders owe their authority to the past. Even if the election of the individual to office is by the votes of a democratic assembly the office itself is traditional and this constitutes its authority with the membership. In religions which have a hereditary priesthood the dependence on the past is obvious. In all religion the question is how the occupant can act in a contemporary manner: whether he can commit his successors to the changes he makes, in particular how the nature of the office itself can be changed. One of the by-products of the discussion of unions between Christian churches is to give this question a thorough airing and, usually, to compel the choice of change as the price of union. The great advantage of tradition when it is as long as that of any of the historic religions is that it gives the chance to appeal to more than one strand in it: it may at times be the reformer's strongest ally.

Before turning to the complicated question of the élites of Christianity a necessarily brief consideration of those of some other religions will point some contrasts. Their future depends not only on their separate and distinctive inner development but on the pressures from without which are common to them all and a world which thrusts them into closer contact with each other.

Religious Leadership in Judaism

Judaism is one of the most instructive religions in the way its élites have developed. The Old Testament shows always two layers of apprehension. Who were the leaders and what did they do? That is the historians' question. But no leadership in any religion has been under such continuous criticism as that of Judaism: *what is* is always brought under the light of *what ought to be*. The Old Testament indeed is not a book which simply records facts: a constant moral and spiritual critique goes on, and there is no continuous history of a single form of religious leadership in Judaism. Early in Jewish history the Levites appear as a priestly tribe, claiming their name and origin from one of the twelve sons of Jacob (or Israel as he was renamed). Moses and Aaron were also among their distinguished forebears. They are therefore not unlike the Brahmins of Hinduism, a sort of caste who act as priests but also may have other occupations; who marry and thus carry on the succession. They seem not to have had a complete monopoly, however, for one of the best known Old Testament priests, Samuel, was not it seems a Levite. As any reading of the Old Testament shows priests were under constant fire from protagonists of reform.

Some of the reformers were themselves priests. They used the re-writing of past history to point the moral of the need for reform. Far from thinking that if sacrificial worship is a good thing there could scarcely be too much of it the priestly reformers tried to limit the priesthood to the family of Aaron and the places where sacrificial worship might be offered to

Jerusalem alone. One may suspect a little monopolistic empire-building, but one must also reckon that priestly reformers were at work in the climate created by what one might well call the second of religious élites of Judaism, the prophets and especially the individual prophets of the eighth century B.C. In their condemnation of the exactions of land-lords and the follies of the people they spared the priests least of all and far from stopping at a castigation of the abuses of sacrificial worship they went on to ask whether a God of mercy and goodness needed such sacrifices at all. Their prophecies were written down – an immensely important step in the history of religion – and thus became a continuing ferment in the life of the people. In passing one may add that they still are. When Mr. Enoch Powell made his attack on the Race Relations Bill in April 1968 a junior minister asked him in the House of Commons 'to remember the words of the prophet Hosea that he who sows the wind shall reap the whirlwind'.

Returning from captivity in the sixth century B.C. the Jews rebuilt the temple at Jerusalem and re-established sacrificial worship there. In A.D. 70 the Romans in a last exasperated and vindictive attack on their troublesome colony destroyed it totally. Priests and sacrifices came to an end. But by that time synagogue worship had become well established and had spread, with the Jews, far beyond the bounds of Palestine.

Jewish professional leadership passed to the Rabbis, teachers learned in the Law, and the Law became the heart of Judaic faith. Although the term Rabbi might be used honorifically for any distinguished teacher, yet it soon became the name of the first élite of any religion to be trained at regular schools and examined in a systematic literary fashion. So Judaism survived the total destruction of one form of worship and of the élites that served it: religious leadership passed to new and different hands but in an unbroken continuity with the past.

Until June 1967 the old city of Jerusalem and the site of the Temple lay as they had ever since A.D. 135, in non-Jewish hands. Yet all over the world Jews were exchanging the traditional Passover greeting 'next year in Jerusalem'. Believer and non-believer alike regarded the wailing wall bordering one side of the immense open expanse that was once covered by the temple buildings and courts as the most revered spot on earth.

In June 1967 in the six day's war the Israeli armies occupied the whole of Jerusalem. The Arab shops and houses that pressed up against the wailing wall were immediately swept away and thousands of excited Jews thronged into the open space. What can it have been like to have felt that the waiting and the prayers of two thousand years were over? Throughout those centuries the Jews have been a people without a home, trying to settle within the nations of the world, frequently subjected to humiliation and to outbreaks of persecution and genocide. For centuries their religion, the worship of the synagogue, the keeping of the Law, the ties of the Jewish family answered for them the question 'Who am I?' In the midst of present despair the religious Jew lived his life by the hope of a future deliverance. But when religious faith declined the Jew was of all men the most exposed to confrontal with *alienation*. He was also the most intelligently and sensitively open to understanding its wider implications: it was not only a Jewish but a human condition. It is not an accident that the men who understood and expounded with such power the themes of man's alienation from his fellow man in society and his alienation from himself, Marx and Freud, were both by origin Jews and neither of them religious believers.

At present the political tensions are so great and the likelihood of fresh violence so apparent that the longer term significance of the return of the Jewish people to Jerusalem gets scant attention. What is clear is the psychological effect of the six day's war among Jews all over the world. Even those who had thought that the future of the Jews lay in the countries in which they lived and who wrote off Zionism as a romantic and expensive adventure have been stirred to an intense feeling of identity with Jews in Israel. Money has been poured out: well-established Jewish families have packed up and left for the unknown hazards of a war-threatened Israel.

The assiduity with which the Israelis study and learn from their own past is evident in their schools. The Bible is taught not only as a religious book and as their literary heritage, made of course far more available to them by the fact that Hebrew is established as the national language, but is regarded, as one teacher said to me, as 'much the most reliable guide there is on how to live in this country'. Special schools for Rabbis have many boys in training on the traditional studies of the scriptures and the Jewish law in all its subsequent intricate development. But who will be the new religious leaders in Israel? What will be their relation to the state and to the strongly secular tradition of most of the Kibbutzim? How will the challenge of the possession of the site of the Temple be met? What about the great mosque that has been on that site since A.D. 685 and contains the famous rock from which it takes its name? Here, according to tradition, Abraham offered Isaac and here the divine disclosure was made that, however fear or devotion might prompt the offering of what is most precious, the sacrifice of another human life is totally unacceptable. This rock is one of the four great sacred sites of Islam and points to common origins shared by three of the world's great faiths, Judaism, Christianity and Islam.

Given peace and leadership no city in the world offers such possibilities for the future development of inter-religious encounter. It is hard to believe that the Jews who have erected over the Dead Sea scrolls one of the most remarkable museum buildings in the world will want to leave the Temple area looking like a cleared bomb site. But anything they do will involve them in an intensification of the dialogue with men of other faiths which at the level of scholarship has already begun, and it will raise new questions: what worship and what religious leaders now?

Many newly independent nations in the world derive a sense of their identity from their past and from the land that belongs to them. Israel's position as a new nation is unique in that while the history of the land has been almost entirely a religious history, the history of the Jews outside that land is one of distinguished leadership in the arts and sciences. For its early development psychology owed more to Jews than to any others. Among immigrants to Israel from the West religion is a vital interest only for a minority.

Jewish religious leadership cannot ignore secular Jewish achievement. Jewish religious scholars are already pointing out a sort of pre-figuring of some modern scientific development in the Jewish religious understanding of nature and of the human person. But scholarly ingenuity of this kind has perhaps only a preliminary role to play in any future cultural development that might make religious thought meaningful to secular Jewish thinking.

The right of a people to survive and to take measures to protect itself against extinction cannot be argued with, but Jewish political nationalism is a new element in Judaism. Victory, even in the short term, has placed on Israel responsibilities towards others which raise once again some of the old questions of Jewish history and Jewish law such as their responsibility towards 'the stranger within the gates' and to the neighbouring states which share the same Semitic origins but are divided now by politics even more than by religion.

That Jewish religious leadership should be insensitive to these moral questions would be out of character. One can see in the future a tension between Israeli nationalism as it might develop and the tradition of universalism which is a glory of the Jewish religious tradition and enshrined in its scriptures. A people of genius cannot have exhausted the stream of religious and philosophical thought. Martin Buber teaching and writing in the Hebrew university in Jerusalem had a world-wide influence of the kind that builds understanding between men of different faiths and his thought has influenced humanist and secular thinking in a way that indicates that there is much more waiting to be done.

The Brahmins

The Brahmins, the priestly caste of Hinduism, have the longest continuous history of any religious élite in the world. The caste system slowly emerged as a means of forming into a stable society the original inhabitants and the Aryan invaders, who began moving into India from the North West in the second millenium B.C. Like the Levites, the Brahmins owed their priestly privileges to their birth: they neither married into other castes nor ate with them nor held any social intercourse with them. Caste means literally 'colour' and paler colour still marks the Brahmin from others, even if he has abandoned the traditional dress, the wearing of the sacred thread, and the characteristic knot of long hair on a shaven head. The doctrine of reincarnation endowed the Brahmin with the status of being the highest form of life to which a man might be born before his escape from the ceaseless round of births. Professor R. C. Zaehner, one of the leading authorities on Hinduism, says that the Brahmins 'arrogated to themselves powers and privileges that it would be difficult to parallel in any other civilization'.[1]

[1] R. C. ZAEHNER, Hinduism (O.U.P., 1962).

By the time the prophets of Israel had arrived at the point of questioning (in the eighth century B.C.) the institution of sacrifice the Brahmins had developed a form of sacrificial worship of immense complexity which was thought to renew the creation and to bring about a unity between man, the world and the creator. Our general modern repugnance to the idea of sacrifice and a lack of discriminating knowledge may easily lead us to think of it merely as 'slaughter', with a rather loathsome emphasis on shedding blood. But in fact some sacrifices do not include the killing of any animals and others use such killings sparingly or as a ritualized form of killing for food. (We go through ritual forms curiously like sacrificial rituals in our culture in the operating theatres of hospitals – dress, cleansing, hierarchies of participants, pre-scribed order of procedure, victim, first ritual incision – all these are recognizable to anyone comparing descriptions of or instructions for, the two.) The elaborate rituals of the Brahmins included altar-building, ceremonial acts and prayers: details for the performance of sacrifices, which might take as much as a year to prepare and complete, are found in the Vedas. One can perhaps regard them as being (before the emergence of sophisticated tools of thought) a way of grappling with the problem of the relation of man in his microcosm, performing his little acts in his short life, to the macrocosm of nature and eternity.

This elaboration of ritual and the dominating place it gave to the priests led to a development away from it. Retiring to the forests with their disciples certain rishis or mystics and sages produced from their meditations, and over a long period of time, the Upanishads. In them the meaning of the sacrifices is transformed into thought upon the relationship of the individual with his limited and earth-bound life to the all-embracing unqualifiable Absolute. What ethical teaching must a man follow and what knowledge must he seek in order to find his release? The period of the formation of the Upanishads ushered in one of the greatest epochs in the history of religion and philosophy. The question of the relation of the individual to the whole, the nature of the human person, the speculative adventure into the nature of reality form part of a great philosophical system which is not only recognized and studied as such all over the world but which, speaking as a living voice, has moulded the thought of some of India's greatest men in modern times.

The way of knowledge and the ascetic ideal were hard for the majority of men. A new or supplementary way began to be popular about the second century B.C. It was centred on two ancient gods of Hinduism, Vishnu and Siva. Rituals and sacrifices became aids to personal devotion and bukti or devotion has been a characteristic element in Hinduism ever since. A new literature, the poetry of the Ramayana and the Mahabharata fed the mind with some of the intellectual content of the Upanishads and, even more, filled the imagination and stirred the heart to worship. Its most perfect part, the Bhagavad-Gita still does. Yet even the Gita with its moving appeal to trust and devotion speaks equally of duty fulfilled through the obligations of caste. To us now, aware of the physical sufferings and the affront to human dignity offered by the caste system to the fifty-five million Indians outside it the positive achievements of a stable social order may not have much appeal. Who can weigh the good and ill of thirty centuries? Nor can the role of the Brahmins over so long a period be assessed *in toto* by a moral yardstick. They survived the great successes of Buddhism in the sixth and fifth centuries B.C. and remained or returned to recreate Hinduism as the religion of India.

Brahmins have always had their critics and detractors: their power and privilege and their immense conservative influence have attracted waves of hatred. I myself have heard political

speeches made by Indian nationalists in the days before
national independence which after consigning the British to
the sea or worse, turned to the 'rivers of blood, Brahmins'
blood, which will flow when the day of independence
dawns'.

The caste system is being slowly eroded by modern customs
and ideas: legislation has opened the temples to all and
abolished the legal, social and educational disabilities of the
outcastes. Popular suffrage and education are giving leadership in the villages to new men. India is constitutionally a
secular state with freedom for the practice of all religion.
Hinduism is the religion of more than eighty per cent of her
people – a great rambling edifice of beliefs and practices. Just
as the British working man is liable to comment that the
middle classes will always get by, whatever the hardships
they complain of, so the Indian watches the age-old facility
of the Brahmin to turn his gifts or influence to profit showing
itself in new ways. In the professions and in business, in
education or administration, as cooks and hoteliers (for
everyone will eat their food) they make their way. And some
will find the money to start the private commercial or technical school for which there are always more than enough
students. Some of them exercise organized political influence
of a conservative character. Some, like the members of the
Rama Krishna Mission turn their attention to social service.
But many Indians engaged in working for social reform in
India today regard religion and particularly Hinduism as a
barrier to the progress they want to see. But so long as
Brahmins adhere to the strictness of their marriage rules,
there will be Brahmins. What their future role in religion
might be as religion and caste cease to be the organizing
principles of society and as those who pursue religious
interests at all rely less and less on their functions, who would
dare predict?

The Religious Elites of Buddhism

If one turns to Buddhism the history of an immensely long-surviving religious élite is repeated. Not priests offering sacrifices and organizing worship but monks are the professional élite of Buddhism. Heredity is not the means of continuing the tradition but rather personal choice. The birth of Buddhism out of the failure of the Gautama to gain enlightenment either from contacts with the Brahmins or from long ascetic discipline and his enlightenment after meditation without any extremes of self-mortification set the whole course of Buddhism towards moderation in conduct and salvation by personal effort. The company of the monks was established in the lifetime of the Buddha, and in spite of the missionary spread of Buddhism over almost the whole of the far east and the diversification of doctrine and scriptures in the course of time, there is a close resemblance everywhere of the monastic life and vocation. With the exception of modern Buddhist developments in Japan where something like a parish life has emerged, the monks seek holiness of life in personal poverty and their only work in the world outside the monastery is that of teaching.

Every Buddhist who takes his religion seriously wants to be wholly devoted to the pursuit of detachment from all desires (the source of human suffering in Buddhist thought), from the impermanent self, from the world which is only what appears, from all concepts of an eternal Being. Many become monks in middle age who have not been able to do so at the permitted age of twenty. Among the monks therefore is the heart and core of Buddhism both as a tradition and as organization. Although they are seeking the way of detachment from the world the missionary intentions and instruction of the founder direct them outwards to propagate the Buddhist way. Thus the work of monks includes not only preserving the tradition but spreading and developing it. The latest Buddhist congress put in hand a large programme for the reorganization of the texts of the Buddhist scriptures to make them an effective instrument for missionary work.

With its emphasis on the transitory nature of life and the illusory character of the world can one speak of a social conscience in Buddhism? In certain places and at times in history the face of Buddhism has been indistinguishable from that of quietism. But among the most cherished principles is that of reverence for life and it is not a long step from the intention not to destroy or harm to a positive interpretation of that principle into active concern to preserve life. Nor is Buddhism necessarily non-political. Its organization has always been flexible enough to adapt to the conditions of different countries to which it has spread and some of its sects have played a political role in the past, especially in China.

The emancipation of Asia from western dominance has brought great changes to the position of Buddhism. Western forms of government, ways of thought and particularly western education purveying western ideas through the medium of a European language swamped indigenous culture and caused many Asians to under-value it. Asian nationalism as an intense self-awareness, cultural, social and ethnic, was a largely unforeseen consequence of independence. The emotions it let loose found expression not only in politics and social action but in a tremendous pride in the past, the language, the art and culture of the people. Buddhism therefore appeared as the animating spirit of much of this cultural heritage: the monasteries had preserved this tradition. Buddhism was present as a living force with new opportunities of helping to shape the future of new countries in continuity with their past.

In Ceylon, independence was followed by a great upsurge

of Buddhist activity. Monks in their yellow robes are to be seen everywhere. Buddhism is militantly anti-western, influential in politics and education and (at least in the short run) destructive of much of value in the country's immediate past. In Burma, Buddhism and the Burmese form of socialism have found a certain harmony in a policy of national withdrawal from the world.

In Vietnam Buddhist monks played a role exceedingly embarrassing to the French colonial government and popular sentiment turned towards them as potential leaders. Buddhism was however organizationally weak: its formlessness made it difficult to crush but also left it without the means of leadership. Nevertheless the monks took part in a transformation of Buddhism, joining in organized efforts to meet the country's needs. Schools, orphanages, social service units, youth organizations, papers and magazines under local Buddhist auspices and linked through Buddhist societies struggled to assist the people of Vietnam to survive a war that for them has gone on for more than twenty years, whose purposes if they were ever known to the ordinary people of the country are now totally obscured. Certain Buddhist monks and nuns deliberately burned themselves in order that their action might be heard of outside their own country and in such a way as to strike horror into the minds of people who then knew little of the sufferings of the Vietnamese people.

In 1966 Thich Nhat Hanh, a Buddhist monk, scholar and poet, made a personal mission to the West to interpret to western peoples the longings of the Vietnamese people for an end to the war. His visit included consultation with the Christian leaders of negro protest movements in the United States; Martin Luther King and others regarded protest for negro rights and against the Vietnamese war as part of one battle on behalf of subject people. The test of the work done in the war by Buddhist monks and lay people will come with the restoration of peace and the need to rebuild a shattered country.

The classes of priests and monks in these three great religions have never been the sole sources of religious thought, still less of virtue and holiness. There have been scholars, poets, saints sometimes of obscure origins. Warriors have had an honourable place and kings a unique one. Kingship is in some sense always a sacred office. Reforms or movements of advance have many times been initiated by kings in the history of these religions. Although their office is sacred, kings have also performed the role, *vis-à-vis* the professionals, of the leading layman: they do not share the professionals' expertise: thus they are with the people as they are also for the people in protecting them against the pretensions of the professionals.

Islam differs very markedly from the other great world religions in being so much a lay brotherhood. Its missionary expansion has been due to the fervour and responsibility of ordinary Muslims in spreading their faith. From the early Middle Ages great Islamic universities were the places where Islamic scholarship developed. Europe became their debtor not only for the recovery of Greek learning but for the mathematics and sciences that they themselves created.

V

THE PROFESSIONALS: CHRISTIANITY

CHRISTIANITY as an organized religion, that is to say as the Church or churches, has owed much in its history to many others than its professional élite: many laymen have been scholars and writers, artists, architects and historians: there have been saints and scientists, philosophers and men of action. The professional élite itself has been shaped by the fact that Christianity did not begin within a single culture or ethnic group but brought people together into a common life from a wide diversity of races, cultures and previous religious backgrounds. Early churches started in houses and involved whole families: women were admitted to the sacred rites of baptism and the eucharist. Special offices and functions emerged within these communities and not in relation to temples or shrines. The ordained ministry was defined and became general while the church was still a persecuted or barely tolerated minority and not after it had entered into partnership with the empire. It is not a caste of individuals born to their status like Brahmins. Every Christian minister, whatever his ultimate status or responsibility may become, is born a layman, even perhaps an outsider to Christianity.

No matter how different their names may be within different churches (clergyman, priest, minister, presbyter, pastor) or even in different contexts in the same church, all the professionals perform recognizably the same functions. Inside their churches they possess authority, duly assigned to them within the recognized tradition and organization. It may be limited by a superior authority here or a democratic assembly there, but their authority enables them to perform the rites of the church and to exercise leadership in their sphere within it. Outside their churches, and regardless of how they themselves may regard each others' ecclesiastical credentials, society tends increasingly to think of them as the same. They are regarded as a class or a profession. Names that were the cause of heated discussion long, or not so long, ago are now applied without a nice discrimination. It is a sign of the growing mutual knowledge of one another and of the common situation they face that this common lot is accepted with little more than an occasional smile on the faces of those who remember other days. But the professionals know – none better – that behind the appearance of likeness are deep differences. They represent divided churches: their office is one of the main points at issue in the continuance of that division.

Any discussion of the functions or reform of the ordained ministry today is bound to take place in an atmosphere created by the criticism that abounds inside and outside the churches. When institutions are powerful they are usually deaf to criticism and when they are weak they are usually unable to act upon it. Probably the churches as institutions are neither as powerful nor as weak as various critics, looking at the same institutions, are saying. Those who prophesy collapse are irritated because it does not happen, while those who work for reform find how enmeshed the ordained ministry is in institutions which have their legal, social, economic and every other aspect, each with a history which cannot be simply wiped out of existence. The difficulty about trying to plot a course by a series of responses to criticism is that much criticism is compounded of opposing elements; some is ill-informed, a little is malicious, a great deal is aimed at general targets like 'authority' or 'élitism', or 'ineffectiveness'. Amid the scorn of the most biting critics outside and the self-flagellations of many church bodies, many sensible things have been said and, in a quiet way, something is being done. For young people however change is not going far or fast enough, especially not for young men in training for the ordained ministry.

The response to all criticism has to be, in general terms, that churches cannot reform themselves or their ministries into becoming something else: but on the other hand they cannot preserve a tradition by wrapping it up and burying it. But these generalizations do not point any way ahead.

What could mark a way ahead would be the emergence of certain priorities which might act as the touchstones of change. It does seem as though three are possible to state. They are – not in order of the importance assigned to them at present but in the order of their emergence as priorities – the following:

First, Christian unity. The sociologist may regard this as 'mergers'. But there is another point of view than his. Growing numbers of Christians are aware of the contradiction between what they proclaim (the unity of mankind in Christ and his love for all) and how they behave to one another in mutual exclusiveness. They are also aware of the new insights into faith and the new opportunities of service in the world that are the direct result of the search for unity over the past fifty years.

Second, the issue of *aggiornamento*. The word used by Pope John XXIII means more than 'bringing the church up to date'; it means renewal of its life and of contact with the world, especially in relation to what is

Thirdly, the issue of world poverty, peace and justice.

This last is taken up in the last chapter.

Local congregations or denominations within a nation would certainly have priorities of their own created by local needs. But once they look beyond their own horizons and begin to ask what the churches as the organized expressions of Christianity ought to be doing in relation to the total as well as the local future, these priorities (and their own share in them) would be likely to emerge. A young man thinking of becoming a professional servant of the church would think of the second as that to which he would hope to make his personal contribution, the third as the battle that a renewed church ought to be fighting in the world and the first as what he hoped he would be able to assume in an international as well as a local sense as the context of his work.

These can be named as priorities because of the focusing of attention on them not only in world bodies like the Second Vatican Council, the World Council of Churches and the Lambeth Conference of the Anglican Bishops (to name only some) and because they make up a large part of the agenda of scores of national councils of churches and figure more and more urgently on those of denominations.

The object here is not to discuss these matters in themselves but rather to ask what effect it would have on the ordained ministry if they were more consistently made the test of action. First however it is necessary to begin where we are with the professional ministries of divided churches.

Professional Ministries

It is not possible to move into a new situation without taking account of the present as it has been made by the past, and that means the past of Christianity and not just of one denomination. The events of history, including those one might wish had not happened, have separated and diversified the ordained ministry. A plea has to be entered here with those who are impatient of all organization and to whom 'structure' is something of a dirty word as though the only structure that could be envisaged were a cage. All institutions from a university to a family need a structure in order to ensure the freedom of their members to associate with one another and with others. The characteristic achievements of the modern world are based on a high degree of organization, not on the lack of it. Outworn and inefficient organization is experienced as repressive because it leaves its members free but does not provide the means by which they can do anything effective: that is the situation of many men in the ordained ministry of the Church of England, described by Leslie Paul in his *Deployment and Payment of the Clergy*.[1] On the other hand efficient organization directed to ends that its members regard as morally wrong or in some other way misdirected is experienced as a restriction of individual freedom. A certain number of Roman Catholic priests and laymen feel like that about certain aspects of their church.

Orthodox and Eastern Churches. The great division of Christendom is not *Catholic* and *Reformed* but *Eastern* and *Western*. The Emperor Constantine announced his espousal of Christianity in A.D. 312. He wanted a united empire and he saw a united church as a means to that end. Summoning and presiding over the Council of Nicaea he established a long tradition in the East of relationship of church and state. When he moved the capital to Constantinople and took the whole administration with him, the Emperor left the Bishop of Rome as the most distinguished citizen of a city still glorious enough to attract every invader. Sacked and desolated, Rome re-found herself, under the guidance of distinguished bishops, as Rome spiritual, with an inheritance from imperial Rome that still persists.

The Eastern churches (plural, for each locality had – and has – its own synod and all are therefore spoken of as *autocephalous* or self-governing churches) respected the see of St.

[1] LESLIE PAUL, *The Deployment and Payment of the Clergy* (Church Information Office, 1963).

Peter and accorded it an honorific first place – no more. In the relations between Rome and the East, time was no healer. Misunderstandings due to differences of circumstance, language and cast of mind (for the Latins never really understood the Greek mentality) burst into open conflicts. The Pope anathematized the ecumenical patriarch; the crusaders, cheated of their aim to recover the Holy Places from Muslim hands, fell upon the church and city of Byzantium and left them so weak as to fall easily into the hands of the Turks.

The Eastern Orthodox were the missionaries to the Slavs, spreading the faith from the Baltic to the Urals. The Orthodox churches of today include those of the Baltic states and Russia, the Balkans, Yugoslavia, and the near east. Closely associated with them as churches whose history is separate from the west are the other Eastern churches: the Armenians, the Copts (Egypt and Ethiopia) and (in a closer relationship short of full communion) the Orthodox Syrian Church founded in South India not later than the sixth century.

Pope Paul VI removed the anathema from the Ecumenical Patriarch at a meeting of the two men in Rome. But that thousand years of estrangement and different history could lead an eminent Orthodox leader to say 'Roman Catholics and Protestants are a quarrel in one house, but Orthodox and Roman Catholics are two different houses'.

The Orthodox world has never had an ecclesiastical language like Latin: the Emperor had plenty of civil servants without drawing on the clergy. It never had an educational system conducted in a language different from that of the ordinary people. It never had a wholly celibate clergy telling married people how to conduct their lives. The bishops were and are drawn from the ranks of the monks, and are unmarried. Some of them may have spent part of their lives as parish priests. The ordinary parish priest is chosen from among the people of the village or township and sent away for some preparation. He then returns to minister: he is married and works at a secular vocation (unless he is in a densely populated parish): he celebrates the liturgy but he does not preach unless he is specially licensed by the bishop to do so. Dioceses are smaller, the bishop usually well-known in his own, from which he does not usually move to any other. In the universities the teaching of theology is done by laymen. Lay orders of men and women help in the parishes, do missionary and social work, teach children, organize youth movements, write and publish books and periodicals.

What is the importance of this remote and for the most part unknown world of Orthodox and Eastern churches to the rest of Christianity? If it did not exist the Roman Catholic Church could rightly say that every Christian body outside her own boundaries was, at however many removes, a historical breakaway from her; that she alone has the continuity of the undivided church and that the only unity is return to Roman obedience. This claim cannot be sustained against the Eastern Churches. They have never been under Rome's jurisdiction[1] and they do not recognize as authoritative the decisions of any church councils that were not councils of the undivided church before the estrangement.

To all Western churches the existence of Orthodoxy is an authoritative radical challenge. To the Orthodox themselves the question of the unity of the Church is a genuinely burning one not for reasons of expediency, and not because they have ever been involved in a Reformation with all its over-hang of guilt. They are concerned because theologically their whole emphasis is that the Church is one: that Jesus Christ founded one church and that there cannot be more than one (except in the geographical sense). They envisage unity as self-

---

[1] The position of those among the Eastern churches that are called Uniats is exceptional: they are self-governing but in communion with Rome.

governing regional churches in communion with one another and acting together. They cannot bring themselves to call most other bodies 'churches' except as a convenience of language: yet it was the Ecumenical Patriarchate which issued (in 1920) the first call to other Christians to take seriously the question of the Church's unity and its present divisions. Their closest contacts, church to church, have been with Anglicans. In the World Council of Churches they and the other Eastern churches represent about a third of the total membership of the Council and their presence and contribution are crucial to the conceptions of unity which have developed in the churches largely as the result of the scholarly work and the constant exchange of information and ideas for which the Council is a forum.

The Roman Catholic Church. Picking up the historical thread once more at the departure of the seat of the empire from Rome to Constantinople one can see how the bishops of Rome were a local rallying point in times of invasion, and how Rome became a centre of pilgrimage as the death-place of the two chief apostles. Churches began to rise. The papacy first gained power in worldly affairs outside Rome as a settler of disputes: legates were sent out either to arbitrate on the spot or to conduct the preliminaries for bringing a case to Rome. The tradition of Rome as a source of law was revived in a new form. The Church developed her own canon law, her own ecclesiastical courts, her own forms of taxation. These provided points of conflict between the Church and civil power, for with them went the claim that the clergy were exempt from the courts and taxes of civil powers. The Church was thus throughout the Middle Ages fashioning itself as a state owning lands, and with temporal as well as spiritual privileges to exact and confer. The territorial possessions of the Vatican vanished in the unification of Italy, but the tiny area of Vatican City still functions as a state. The concordats made between the Vatican and the governments of states have the status of treaties; the Vatican both receives and appoints ambassadors and often deals directly with governments. The Pope therefore combines in his person the functions of a head of state; bishop of the diocese of Rome; foremost bishop of his church; father of a vast company of 'the faithful', for whose lives he demonstrates in various ways a personal interest; and the voice of his church to the world. The structure of the Roman Catholic Church still bears vestiges of its history as 'a state between and within states'. It has the feudal remains of hierarchies of individuals owing loyalty and expecting protection: it has the kind of Tudor civil service that a Cecil would recognize: it has flashes – more than flashes – of superb modernity.

Within an institution with such a history (simplified by brevity to the point of caricature) the Roman Catholic bishops and clergy work. Most of them were recruited as boys and began their education for the ministry at seven or eight. In their seminaries the basic outlines of their training have not changed since the Middle Ages. Some in addition attend courses in universities on a wide variety of subjects, as also do nuns. What must strike any observer about the Roman Catholic 'professionals' is the great range from the simple parish priest who spends his life in a village to the head of a great religious order. They are both closer down among the poor and more like the big organization-men of the modern world than the professionals of any other religious body. Anson Phelps Stokes in his monumental work *Church and State in the United States*, speaks of the Roman Catholic Church as one of the few democratizing forces of the Middle Ages for, he says, there was no boy so poor that he might not one day become pope, or so humbly born that he might not become the senior officer of a great state. This escalation is still possible and indeed frequent in the church which provides within its own organization all levels of education for those destined for high office.

The differences between countries are too great to describe in any detail. It is a far cry from the close-knit parish life of the Irish in a poor part of Liverpool to the state of affairs in Latin America where religion is a part of the culture but there is far less parish life or personal devotion. In a Catholic country like Brazil there is one priest to eighty thousand people, a high proportion of them coming from outside the country. Most other parts of Latin America are also heavily dependent on the religious orders to send priests from outside the continent for schools and universities and for parochial work in the cities and missionary work among the vast Indian population, and nuns for schools and hospitals.

Everything about Rome is touched with an element of its universalism. On the counters of Irish shops stand the collecting boxes for the mission in Korea or Japan, the hospital in Nigeria, the school somewhere else. The great religious orders, men and women, are in some ways more highly organized than Rome itself, with power to direct their members to any work anywhere. It is they who carry on the mission of the church in Asia and Africa and elsewhere, and its vast commitments in education everywhere. Nobody who talks about the Roman Catholic Church can speak of more than the tip of an iceberg.

National Churches. In the ministries of the churches which stem from the Reformation one sees degrees of continuity and of break with the traditions of the past. James I, who was always sour towards the Scottish and English Presbyterians, remarked that 'new presbyter was but old priest writ large' and so voiced a lay as well as a royal opinion. The only spiritual authority in whose name the reformers could challenge those practices of the church of Rome which they deemed to be wrong or defective was that of Holy Scripture. I have already described how the shape and use of church buildings was changed to give visible expression to the authority of the Bible in worship and to the enlarged role of preaching and diminished role of sacraments in some of them. The Reformation also changed the structure of the professional ministry in its internal relationships of authority and its relation to civil power.

Mixed up with the reformers' quarrel with the church of Rome was the struggle of a number of European nations against large imperial powers. Churches and nations went through these crises together and the new or refashioned churches bore the marks of this in their subsequent constitutions. All the churches which broke with papal supremacy but retained the historic episcopate became national or state churches, Lutheran or Anglican (the Scandinavian countries, the German states and England). But the reverse was not true: some national churches emerged, like the Church of Scotland or the Reformed Church of the Netherlands (which is not a *state* church) or the churches of some of the German states, which were not episcopal in form.

The episcopal churches retained all the hierarchy of authority except the papacy, and the organization of geographical dioceses and parishes. (Parishes, but not dioceses, were also part of the civil organization in England.) They also retained some of the clerical privileges and immunities that had belonged to the church of Rome before the Reformation: that is why there are twenty-four bishops in the House of Lords and why clergymen of the Church of England are not liable for military service. On the other hand the state gained wholly for itself what it had disputed with the papacy before the Reformation, namely the appointment of bishops. To have 'replaced' the pope by the king is regarded now by

Roman Catholics and perhaps by many others as a monstrous act. It also seemed so to many at the time and was the hardest part of the Reformation for them to accept in conscience. For others it was less so: the papacy was a worldly office: kings were still regarded as sacred persons and there was adequate confirmation of this in the Bible. Though it is hard to see Henry VIII of England personally in that light, his title 'Defender of the Faith', borne by all his successors, was given to him not by a Protestant parliament but by Pope Leo X for his treatise defending the seven sacraments against Luther.

The non-episcopal national churches were more radical in their reform but in their connection with the state they re-interpreted some aspects of the hierarchy of the Roman Catholic Church. They abolished the hierarchy of persons in the ministry and substituted a single order of ministry, so that no minister has any precedence or authority over another. Reformed (Presbyterian) authority is expressed instead in what the Church of Scotland calls 'a hierarchy of courts': the local court of minister and elders is the Kirk session, the next above it is the court of the Presbytery (a small geographical grouping) and at the national level is the General Assembly of the Church of Scotland. The use of the word *courts* is interesting in that it retains the legal connotations of the past. None of these courts is complete or able to take decisions without the presence and vote of the elders. Elders are not simply laymen for, although they cannot administer the sacraments and are not the ordained ministry, they receive their office (which in the case of some of them is for life) by a form of institution referred to as 'ordination'. Instead of being involved with the civil administration at many levels as all established churches were at their beginning and in form continue to be, the Church of Scotland has an autonomous system of government related to the state at the highest level of its structure. This is symbolized by the presence of the High Commissioner at the General Assembly as the representative of the crown,[1] but not presiding over it. Its rights and privileges are recognized in the Act of Union of England and Scotland, 1707.

The General Assembly has been for four hundred years the nearest thing to a Scottish Parliament, a powerful voice of opinion (though not of civil legislation or executive responsibility). This explains the strong reaction of popular opinion (which certain sections of the Scottish press have had no difficulty in blowing up to even more violent expressions) to suggestions of union of the Church of Scotland with the Episcopal Church of Scotland on terms that would introduce bishops into the Church. The report[2] of the conversations between the Church of England, the English Presbyterians and the two churches in Scotland was dubbed from the moment of publication 'the Bishops' Report' and assigned in popular imagination a place with 'the bishops' war' (1639) of bitter memory. Later, even sober theologians were writing about the ecumenical movement as a thinly disguised attempt to 'Anglicanize' the Church of Scotland.

The decline of religion and of the national authority of the General Assembly of the Church of Scotland may well be factors in the rise of Scottish nationalism. The anxiety of spokesmen of the Church of Scotland that the discussion of a parliament for Scotland should not become a party political issue is well-founded. Whatever the weaknesses of the General Assembly from the national point of view, one of its strengths has been its freedom to voice opinions on

[1] As this book goes to press the Queen has announced that she will not appoint a High Commissioner for 1969, but will be present in person.

[2] *Relations between Anglican and Presbyterian Churches* (S.P.C.K., 1957).

national issues (often conveyed to the public or presented to the whole Assembly by its influential 'Church and Nation' committee), without being saddled with party politics. The Church of Scotland ministry expresses two strong traits in Scottish history and character: its passion for equality (expressed by Burns as 'a man's a man for a' that') and for education; taken as a whole it probably is the best educated ministry there is.

Free Churches. The term 'Free Church Ministers' is frequently used in England to describe the ministers of Presbyterian, Baptist, Congregational, Methodist and sometimes Unitarian churches. The term replaces the older use of 'nonconformist'. It has a certain usefulness as meaning 'non-episcopal' or 'not established' but it is not a description equally applicable to all either in terms of their origins, or in terms of the worship and organization of their churches. The union of Congregationalists and English Presbyterians, to be complete in 1970/71 and the negotiations for union between the Methodists and the Church of England will make the term out of date.

The largest of the English free churches is the Methodist Church of Great Britain, constituted by a union of Methodist bodies in 1932. It is ruled by a yearly conference, the successor of that founded by Wesley himself, of which half the members are ministers elected by the forty-six Synods. These 325 ministers decide all matters concerning the ministry, including the 'posting' of ministers to their charges which they hold for a minimum of three and norm of five years. The forty-six districts into which the church is divided regionally are not unlike the dioceses of the Church of England, especially since their chairmen were made ministers without a special local charge and therefore more like bishops in function. Within the districts the circuits group local churches. There are more churches than ministers in a circuit and therefore many services are conducted by lay preachers, men and women, and the circuit plan organizes in detail how this shall work. Methodists have a deserved reputation as a close-knit body caring for their own members and as a body with a strong social conscience. Their highly centralized organization enables them to find the means to many special activities and for church extension.

Methodists in America constitute (with a membership of ten millions) the largest of all the denominations with the exception of the Roman Catholics. Their early superintendents assumed the name of bishop which is retained and is used where they have founded churches overseas. Methodists in Canada have already united with others to form the United Church of Canada and in South India Methodists are part of the Church of South India. This last is the only place where they are united with Anglicans so far.

*

Something has already been said in chapter II about the influence of the movements for radical reform on worship and organization and therefore on buildings. If one looks now at the organization of their ministries perhaps two or three points can be briefly made: further discussion will be found in other books.[1] Many Baptist church buildings look very much like other free church buildings except for the presence of the baptistry, usually covered by a platform except when it is opened for adult baptisms. The local organization of the congregation with its control over its own affairs does not differ much from that of Congregationalists. But it is just that exception that constitutes the difference. Baptists in this country co-operate more closely with other denominations than they do in many other parts of the world, and therefore the difference is obscured. In the United States, for example,

[1] See Bibliography.

while the Northern Baptist Convention is a member of the World Council of Churches, the Southern Baptists who number some six million stand aloof. In Russia there are probably at least two million Baptists. Not church government but the understanding of the sacrament of baptism is the dividing line between Baptists and other believers. For them, personal faith must always precede baptism. This runs counter to the practice of Christianity from early times and to the practice of most churches today. However, the custom of infant baptism cannot be justified by a strict application of the letter of the New Testament. Rising sects pushing out and making adult converts practise adult baptism and use it as a form of witness. Any who base their practices on a strict application of scripture without regard to tradition tend to be 'baptists' in principle though they do not necessarily have the name 'baptist' in their titles. They are a vast and varied company in the world.

But that is not the whole story. Many Baptist congregations, especially those long established, do not enforce adult baptism as a rule that must apply to all members. Nor on the other hand do the great historic churches regard infant baptism as a principle: they too baptize adults and will do so increasingly as the baptism of infants ceases, if it does, to be a part of the cultural pattern. The Church of England has recently recognized adult baptism as the norm, and the baptism of infants as derived from it. All churches recognize that in exceptional circumstances lay people may validly baptize. It is increasingly common for churches to point to baptism as the already existing sign of a present unity among them: the future of relationships with Baptists is not a closed one.

The Role of World Confessions and Communions

Separate ministries are the test of the existence of separate churches. For example, John Wesley, failing to get the Church of England to ordain men to serve converts in the American colonies (which in colonial days were part of the jurisdiction of the diocese of London) took the decision to ordain men himself. Only then did what had been a society within the Church of England start on its way to becoming a separate church out of communion with the Church of England. Separate self-governing churches can however arise without a breach in communion. For example, many groups of emigrants to Australia or the Americas received their ministries from abroad until the parent church recognized their independence and they became self-governing bodies. Communion with their parent churches and with others of the same confessional grouping continues unquestioned until the possibility of uniting with other local churches of a different confession arises: then relationships begin to go into the melting pot. There are forty such sets of union conversations going on in the world now.

Churches of the Reformed and Lutheran traditions speak of their world-wide connections as 'confessional' groupings, because a number of the older among them were originally constituted as churches by the agreement to abide by a certain statement of their position, such as the Westminster Confession, the Heidelberg Confession and so on. Anglicans on the other hand speak of the Anglican Communion. The calling in 1858 of the first Lambeth Conference of all Anglican bishops gave it its first corporate (but purely consultative) voice. The latest Lambeth Conference (1968) contained representatives of churches in communion with the Anglican churches, as well as observers from others. Methodists, Congregationalists and Baptists have world alliances or councils.[1]

[1] The first Christian world bodies were not church bodies. The Evangelical Alliance was the first (1846): it spoke of itself as having an

World-wide bodies of the same confessional groupings normally discuss the union schemes into which some of their constituent churches may be moving, in order to ensure that unity in one place does not create further divisions elsewhere: this may be a decisive step in some decisions. The 1968 Lambeth Conference encouraged the Anglican participants in union schemes for North India and for Ceylon to take the imminent final steps without fear of being put out of communion with others. When the proposed union of the Church of England with the Methodists was discussed a narrow corner was turned by the intervention of the Metropolitan of the Anglican Church of North India, Pakistan, Burma and Ceylon, Bishop Lakdasa de Mel. A small but vocal minority in the Church of England was convinced that the proposed service of reconciliation which would unify the ministries of the two churches and bring about immediate inter-communion was, by unclear wording, implying a re-ordination of Anglicans or else no re-ordination of Methodists, either of which would be unacceptable to them. An amendment avoiding all comment on the issue was on the point of being passed when the Metropolitan, who has the looks and presence of a cultured Sinhalese Buddhist, from which stock he springs, and the speech of a cultivated Englishman of the old school, leapt into the debate and successfully urged the Conference 'not to keep our Methodist brethren dangling any longer'. He was not speaking as an irresponsible voice from outside, for his own church would be affected by what happened. He was also making a point of principle: that if the Church of England could make comments on unions contemplated by other Anglican churches it must take the same medicine in regard to its own.

'ecumenical basis'. Then came the World Alliance of Y.M.C.A.'s (1855).

This is only one of hundreds of possible illustrations of the way in which a world perspective alters views in the churches. Sociologists looking at the local scene and regarding unions between churches as mergers have no idea of the world-wide repercussions that unions or failures to unite have, nor of the complex of motivations that work to persuade churches to enter into discussions with others about union: which ones they approach, why and when.[1]

Separate ministries constitute separate churches: unions of churches therefore mean *at least* uniting their ministries: intercommunion between churches means a mutual recognition of the validity of ministries, and this can only be achieved by crossing the same theological and historical barriers as for union, while avoiding the organizational ones. Since the final decisions usually have to be taken by bodies formed mainly or entirely of the ordained ministers of churches, they are discussing their own function and status when they discuss whether and how their church could unite with any other.

Priorities for the Future

Unity. The term 'Christian unity' is used to express comprehensively *all* aspects of a recovery of oneness between Christians or churches, while 'union' means the uniting of two or more churches to form one church.

One of the strongest pressures towards unity is the desire to end the scandal that Christians are not able to receive holy

---

[1] It is a pity that Dr. Bryan Wilson in his book *Religion in Secular Society* allowed himself to be persuaded by an unpublished PhD thesis into identifying the meaning of 'ecumenical' with 'unions' and the origins of the ecumenical movement with an early merger of Methodist splinter groups. As he would have seen by reference to the history of the ecumenical movement the concern of the Christians with the *world-wide* fellowship (the original meaning of 'ecumene' is 'the inhabited world') preceded their willingness even to discuss their divisions, let alone to consider union.

communion from all Christian ministers, nor are ministers all allowed to give it to them. Lay people are affected by opposing rules of divided churches in other ways also, and most acutely in mixed marriages: the professionals are affected by them in their work. The scandal of division at what is called the sacrament of unity so shocks some Christians that they are prepared to put conscience above the rules of any church, their own or another. Others believe such actions are a greater scandal. The Archbishop of Canterbury in a somewhat elliptical saying struck what some would think the right balance between discipline and freedom: 'institutions must be something and individuals must be free'.

Union *as a goal* means less and less. Aiming at union for its own sake does not solve the basic problem, what churches ought to be doing and being. It may even divert attention from that issue. *As a means* it is more urgent than ever, so urgent that in many ways it just has to be taken for granted as a future reality. Many actions must be done, many refrained from, in the belief that there will be a closer union of the churches: for example, begin training together men for the ministry and stop putting up separate denominational schools; tackle local needs as the local situation demands and not as denominational separation dictates; use intercommunion wherever allowed as a way of preparation not as a way of avoidance of the issue of closer union. These seem the type of demand that comes when groups of professionals (and many lay people too) realize that, for example, the needs of an inner city or a new housing area or an area of racial tension or an underprivileged group cannot be met by uncoordinated denominational effort. But church authorities which are not more and more putting themselves out to face the real issues of today will leave some of their most devoted and gifted professionals to labour under unnecessary frustrations and disabilities. But remote denominational control would not be improved on if replaced by cumbersome local ecumenical machinery: the lesson of the fast-growing, largely independent sects has to be taken.

The Roman Catholic Church is not a party to any negotiations for union with other churches. Quite apart from questions of doctrine, the Roman Catholic Church as a universal church with a centralized authority could not enter into negotiations with national or regional churches except on the basis of absorbing another church into itself. 'The gate of the sheepfold stands open' said Pope Paul VI on his visit to Bethlehem, the first of his journeys outside Rome. He was heard as saying 'the way to unity is by submission': that is unacceptable to other churches. The future might produce delegated powers from Rome to regional colleges of bishops for intercommunion or even union in certain circumstances or church to church relationships of a new kind. That is all unpredictable. But the principle of acting as though the future held other possibilities than stalemate still holds good, not least because fellow Christians need one another if they are to live effectively in a world that is the same for them all, a world that even the most powerful ecclesiastical authority can no longer command.

Renewal of Life and of Contact with the World

The second Vatican Council was called by Pope John XXIII so that Roman Catholic bishops (who are related to the centre but do not enjoy much communication between the parts) might discuss together pressing issues for the church in the modern world. His object was not to impress the world but to start on a wide scale, if agreement could be found, a process of *aggiornamento* in the Church. The most important document to issue from it was the Dogmatic Constitution on the Church – the first official statement on the church ever made by the Roman Catholic Church. Many other documents were concerned with ecumenical relations, with the church in the world, with the laity, liturgy and a number of other topics.[1]

To those outside, some of the most important things about the council were not the documents. The atmosphere created by the Council was one of immediate warmth. A liberal and forward-looking outlook turned out to be far more wide-spread among the bishops than anyone, including themselves, had suspected. All over the world barriers went down between Roman Catholics and 'separated brethren'. Reforms in worship were immediate: the vernacular could be used for saying mass: lay people were not only permitted but encouraged to read the Bible by the provision of new translations and the sanction of the use – with reservations – of 'protestant' Bibles.

It was therefore widely felt that as other Christians, and especially the full-time servants of the churches, struggled to get out of some of their enclosures and into closer contact with the world, Roman Catholics would not only be with them, but might in some respects take the lead along the way to *aggiornamento* that Pope John had pointed. In October 1967 a large congress of the Lay Apostolate called specifically to discuss the lay movements of the church in their relations with the world engendered the same hopes. Obviously the laity were straining to take responsible action, and among them were persons of outstanding gifts ready to be used in the service of the church and the world. The establishment in Rome of a Council for the Laity and the appointment of the important papal commission on Justice and Peace gave great encouragement.

[1] The full text of all the documents of the council, with a Roman Catholic and a non-Roman Catholic comment on each, is published in one volume by Geoffrey Chapman, 1967.

Shortened versions of the more important ones, including those mentioned here, are published by The Grail at 2s. 6d. each.

It was always stressed by the wise to the over-enthusiastic that the period after the Vatican Council would have to see consolidation: that conservative opinion which had taken some shocks would have to have time to recover its breath. Adjustments were to be expected. But then doubts began to rise. A statement at the end of the Year of Faith, coinciding with the opening of the Fourth Assembly of the World Council of Churches (July 1968) stressed the differences of doctrine that separated the churches: that perhaps was wise, as perhaps was the clarification of rules for association between Roman Catholics and others: at any rate they were much more liberal than the situation before the Council. On mixed marriages the old position was recorded. Where was the new Rome?

This question came to a head with the papal encyclical on birth control of August 1968. It rejected the strong plea the Lay Congress made a year before that within a doctrinal framework laid down by authority, married couples should be free to decide for themselves whether and how to limit the size of their families, using medical advice. The theological arguments produced by the Pope in his encyclical ran counter to the advice tendered to him by his own official theological commission on the subject and were regarded by many theologians as specious.

The crisis precipitated was not about contraception so much as about authority and the role of the different parts of the church within it. The laity did not get the responsibility that its more articulate and educated members were asking for: but some did not want it, and millions of Roman Catholic peasants in Asia and Latin America and elsewhere had not heard of contraception. When they do it will be as a government-sponsored effort at population control rather than as an issue of responsibility in the church. Were the educated laity asking (not on their own behalf only, but for the millions in advance of their having to make a decision about their loyalties) for something impossible until a prior issue of principle is made clearer? That issue is *in what sense* in Roman Catholic doctrine the laity are a part of the Church.

The term 'the people of God' has been used recently by many leading Roman Catholic laity: it formed part of the title of the Congress already referred to. In its biblical meaning 'the people (*laos*) of God' signifies the whole Church. The use of the term is therefore disliked by some members of the hierarchy because it blurs as they think, the distinction between the hierarchy and the faithful and leads back to what are regarded as dangerous Protestant ideas of democracy which the hierarchy was, at the time of the Counter-Reformation, greatly strengthened to combat. In Roman Catholic canon law the laity have always been negatively defined as those who have 'no part in the power of jurisdiction and especially of holy order'. Does this mean, some Roman Catholics ask, that lay people may never take any part in the making of decisions that vitally affect them but do not touch the clergy at all? Those who ask the question would not regard verbal answers as adequate.

If this encyclical tells the laity that responsibility for decision-making even in the intimate relationships of man and wife is not for them, what does it do to the clergy, the laity's pastoral advisers and confessors? This perhaps is the real crisis: not that it causes but that it clarifies the situation that a number of Roman Catholic priests feel themselves to be in: *are we not to think for ourselves?*

Why should this be a crisis now and not at other times in the past? The reason may be that in a static or more or less static society people's lives were lived in accordance with two regularities: those of nature and those of a society organized by roles: rulers and ruled, masters and servants, husbands and wives, parents and children. Rights and duties were balanced and infringements clear. The area of personal choice is limited. In such societies the priest too had and has – for such societies still exist – his role. In a modern mobile society there is less dependence on the regularities of nature and individuals perform many different roles including new ones. Somehow the individual has to learn to harmonize all these different roles and pass from one to another and in particular to play out the chief of them – those of family and work – in radically changed and changing conditions. Education is increasingly directed towards helping people to live in many worlds and provides them with some of the knowledge and skills they need for making their choices. If the parish priest is to live with them surely he needs to share this kind of life and to have his own comparable area of making choices and exercising responsibility? If evidence is asked for this opinion it is perhaps to be found in Joan Brothers' book *Church and School*,[1] a Roman Catholic sociologist's study of parishes in Liverpool which shows how secondary education breaks up the close traditional pattern of relationship of priest and family as older children acquire new needs and new attitudes.

An aspect of the problem of authority in the Roman Catholic church is precisely the church's universalism. One rule is promulgated for people in situations as different as New York and Mauritius. It might be argued that the educated laity of an advanced country have to wait for (and indeed might help to hasten) the economic and educational development of the poor before changes of rules are made. But wherever there is over-population this is in itself a sign that one of the big regularities of nature has already been interfered with by man; death has been brought under some control. And Christian hospitals, dispensaries and health programmes all over the world have helped to do this. The

[1] JOAN BROTHERS, *Church and School* (University of Liverpool Press, 1964).

priest in the poor area, especially if he is one of the few leaders that the people possess and is more educated than they, may need also an area of freedom to do what from his intimate knowledge of the situation he knows ought to be done in that place.

The matter of the papal encyclical on birth control has been used here to illustrate a general point about the future: the possibility that living by rules has to give way to living by principles with a greater freedom of interpretation. This means closer contact between professionals and lay people and in new relationships of openness. It means constant re-education for the professionals, parallel to the constant re-training that modern industry demands.

The crisis of authority has only just begun. We may be on the edge of a new reformation in which those who protest and object do not leave the church but stay to face the issue out. The greatest lesson Roman Catholics have for others is their loyalty: but its corollary is the warning of the deviousness of thinking and the pressure on personal freedom and integrity that can result from making loyalty the absolute value.

For other Christians the experience of the period after the Vatican Council would seem to indicate that *aggiornamento* cannot be led by Roman Catholics nor proceed without them. It has to be followed along a number of different lines, some within the churches, some with others, some in vigorous co-operation with non-Christians. The radical overhaul of organization, especially of the parochial system, the closing of many more buildings, the reduction of numbers of services, changes in the training of the professionals and their re-training, must proceed faster. But bringing the churches up to date cannot consist in doing whatever the *avant-garde* in the world does (only several years later). Churches will be renewed and will also serve the world best if they look not to the world but to their own faith as criterion. What use to the world is a religion exactly like it? To love and serve God and their neighbours means a new depth to personal religion, a new and more neighbourly relationship with other Christians and other men, and a disciplined life without which nobody and no group is really effective or has any right to speak. As agents of these developments the professionals have to leave the pulpits which surround them like shadowy structures and connect the personal faith that thousands are trying to win for themselves with the great traditions of religion whose riches need a key.

A last word in this chapter might turn reflection back to the position of the monk in Buddhism. A monk is what a layman would like to be in order to fulfil his personal religious search. This element is almost wholly lacking in modern talk about the role of the professionals in Christianity. So much talk of relevance, worldly involvement and service for others; so much fear of being – or being thought to be – 'holier than thou' masks the aspect of the personal search for faith and holiness. Men and women respect and need the example of such lives, and while they will neither seek nor find them only among the professionals, it would be a perilous future that could not find them there.

VI

ADHERENTS

IT is sometimes suggested by those who are dissatisfied with the teaching of religion in schools that it would be better to stop all religious teaching to young children and to teach older children about several religions, leaving them to make their own choice. There are several good and practical reasons for teaching about other religions than Christianity in our schools. The situation created by immigration – unforeseen at the time of the 1944 Act – with the demands it makes on understanding and tolerance is one such reason. Another is that we live in one world with other religions. But that a lesson or two a week on a few of the world's great religions could result in realistic, informed and meaningful *choice* of *a religious faith* seems most unlikely and the expectation that it could be done is probably based on an insufficiently thought-out conception of what belonging to and believing in a religion actually means.

What is being an adherent of a religion? That is a modern question, in origin a Western question, probably a post-Enlightenment question. No society in which man's view of nature and of human society is inextricably tied up with his view of the holy can ask the question. It becomes insistent only in a world like our own where there is unbelief and religious pluralism and where society has many organizations that have little or nothing to do with religious belief or practice and expects religious belonging to be like belonging to them.

States define the meaning of an adherent for purposes of

their own: they may for example fix a minimum age for participation in religious rites or demand proof of numbers before allowing the use of buildings. Religious authorities often find it hard to make a definition: what about children, for example, or those in regular attendance who do not join, or joining do not attend? If infant baptism is widely practised how do numbers compare with other bodies that have rites only for the admission of adults? Only in 1902 did an official report of the Church of England[1] suggest that social changes and legislation had 'made it necessary for the first time to define membership of the Church of England'; only in 1951 was it first made legally possible to leave the Church of Sweden, of which every Swede was a member by birth, without joining another religious body.

For religions other than Christianity – which did begin as a *society*, definitions are even more difficult. People act and think in a certain way and thus are the followers of a religion. Social pressure and the force of custom keep them in that way rather than an authority. 'Rationalist theorists of religion' writes Professor Evans-Pritchard 'have generally treated conceptions and beliefs as the essentials of religion, and regarded the rites only as external extensions of these. But, as we have already heard from others, it is action which dominates the religious life'.[2]

*

I would distinguish three basic aspects of adherence: the cultural, the societal and the personal. All these words are

[1] JOINT COMMISSION OF THE CONVOCATIONS, *The Position of the Laity in the Church*, 1902 (Republished by the Church Information Office, 1956).
[2] E. E. EVANS-PRITCHARD, *Theories of Primitive Religion* (O.U.P., 1965), p. 62. Although he is talking about primitive religion his words are worth hearing in relation to all religion. *Acting in a certain* way is what most people think of as religion and the rigid framework of

used in a variety of common or technical usages and have different meanings according to context. I mean by the first participation in the external rites and ceremonies once practised universally in a tribe, nation or larger group and still widely practised; the archaeologist or historian of religion would call this the *cultus*. By the second I mean the group voluntarily chosen, within which one can speak of adherents as *members* (which is not possible in relation to the first meaning) who are bound together by religious commitment of some kind. Thirdly by the *personal* I mean the inner commitment of an individual to a religious belief and way of living which he may or may not be able to express in membership of any group, or which may be different from that of the group to which he belongs or from the rites and ceremonies that he takes part in.

I will take up the last of these first. At first glance 'personal belief' and 'adherence' are contradictory terms, the one implying originality, the other conformity. Even if this were a right identification, however, every adherent's beliefs would be his own in the same sense as every person's thoughts are his own, although they have no particular originality about them. But it seems that between one adherent and another of the same group there are significant variations in the content of religious belief and experience. Concluding the summary of data obtained from a study of the variations of belief between members of distinctive sub-groups in Christianity, Dr. Owen Brandon writes: 'When all the work of plotting distinctions and of calculating statistics has been done,

---

defined boundaries of belonging is alien to many of them. Under persecution or pressure of proselytism by a more powerful religious influence there will often be a closing of the ranks, but the tendency is to relax the strict controls and to take the most inclusive definition of belonging as normative when not under stress, and the least inclusive when there is the fact or the fear of pressure and possible disintegration.

the data stand as a monument to the truth of the inwardness and personal nature of religion for the individual.'[1] One would therefore expect greater variety among those not belonging to any religious group although the expectation would need to be qualified by the observation that they would be likely to have less material out of which to make their religious beliefs.

It seems therefore that personal religion is an element in adherence: probably as people depart from adherence to a group they retain or remake some of its elements. Some ex-Christians seem to remain puritans or catholics or calvinists in temperament and even in the secular forms of belief and conduct. Possibly also personal belief plays different roles in different cultures and at different times.

Emphasis on personal religion is a strand in all the world's religions. Each man makes his own act of devotion and prayer, his sacrifice or his pilgrimage. The monk in the religious order repents of his own sins. Within Hindu culture it is impossible to speak of 'conforming', for it is difficult to see who and what would be the conformers and that which is conformed to. Credal statements and an authority to impose acceptance of them are pre-conditions of the possibility of conformity. But with our present knowledge of the personal nature of religious belief one can look back and see the varieties of religious response to the same doctrines. William James[2] was the first to apply a psychologist's understanding to the varieties of religious experience and to the temperamental differences that underlie them. Authority prevented certain expressions of religious experience and canalized religious feeling into certain channels, but that these

[1] OWEN BRANDON, *Christianity from Within* (Hodder & Stoughton, 1965), p. 57.

[2] WILLIAM JAMES, *The Varieties of Religious Experience* (Longmans, 1902).

varieties existed can be adduced from evidence. That individuals with strongly personal expressions of belief and a particularly vivid personal experience were highly influential in setting in motion new trends in old religious societies can be abundantly illustrated from the history of religion. Saint Francis exemplifies perfectly such an influence and there are comparable examples in every religion. But can the richness of the possibilities that individuals hold within themselves for the development of religion ever reach a full expression under the dominance of a conception of a fixed and unchanging doctrine? John Henry Newman was the first to argue that in fact doctrine *does* change with time: his predecessors who studied the question said that what changed was the expression of it.[1] Newman wrote his *Essay on the Development of Christian Doctrine* at the time of his conversion to the Roman Catholic Church in 1845. He was one of the very first thinkers in any field to use the concept of development which is so readily taken for granted today. The gradual acceptance of such a point of view changes the context within which the individual adherent holds his beliefs: it becomes worth working and waiting for change.

The Reformation broke up the cultural and religious unity of Christendom and brought a new emphasis into religion accompanying the growth of modern individualism. The causal relationships between religious changes and the emergence of the new class of the entrepreneurs have been much debated. Certainly there are signs of the growth of capitalism earlier than the fifteenth century, and the medieval heretics were the first who challenged the undisputed authority of the church over individual belief by an appeal to the scriptures and an assertion of the right to interpret them for oneself. After the Reformation there was a far greater tendency for men to become the arbiters of right and wrong in their own

[1] OWEN CHADWICK, *From Bossuet to Newman* (C.U.P.).

belief and conduct, but the need to belong seemed as strong as ever and took new forms as men founded or joined new groups and went out to seek converts. The terms of membership and the degree of conformity demanded by many of the new groups were as strong or stronger than those of the Catholic Church their fathers had left.

When people speak of having a religion of their own today they usually mean something different from freedom within a religious cultural pattern or freedom to join an established group. Religious leaders are saying that no religious faith is effective that is mere conformity and that the young adult must be free to make his own choice: but many of the young adults are replying that the expectation that they will choose is what must be challenged. The necessity to prove to themselves that they were not brainwashed by their teachers or conditioned by their parents or dominated by their pastors brings about an all but irresistible impulse to withdraw to a position of minimum open commitment to any formal acts of religious belonging or believing or behaving. Another factor in the steady withdrawal over the years has been the widespread belief that religion has been discredited by science. The prestige of science is such that priority of credence attaches to any claim advanced in its name. Neither education nor any other agency has effectively bridged the gap between them. To break with adherence in the sense of belonging to a religious group is easy: but to break with cultural belonging is more difficult or even impossible. What happens is partly a break by the individual, partly a change in the culture brought about by the pressure of individual actions.

At the same time there is the opposite phenomenon of a generation brought up to conform to irreligion showing signs of independence of thought and readiness to discuss what are certainly religious questions in largely non-religious language. A third element among the younger generation are those who have received a new kind of religious upbringing, far more open to their contemporaries, ready to join them in service to others and much better prepared than any former generation to see the dialectic of religious commitment in a continuous response to changing situations.

One comes in the end to thinking of the religious beliefs of thousands upon thousands of individuals as both providing a faith for themselves and modifying the *cultus*. The general opinion is that the influence of religion upon the cultus is declining; that society and even life itself are being secularized. But the concept of 'secularization' is one that still needs more exploration: it may not be as valid as it is thought to be. The individual shows signs of wanting to hit back against the forces that by secularizing his life deprive large areas of it of any meaning. There used to be, for example, a close link between work and worship. This is now broken: most people find work as such meaningless. This may indeed be the effect of secularization – to render that part of life that it touches meaningless and the person threatened by it vulnerable to total meaninglessness. Therefore it may be a question of survival for the human spirit; of whether individuals have kept in their hearts enough of the feeling for religion to help them to fight back. The role of the outstanding individual is therefore of crucial importance. Institutions do not renew themselves, but individuals can be, as always, the unexpected sources of new life.

Adherence as Participation in the Religious Cultus

Since nobody chooses his parents, or the nation, state or culture into which he is born, there is a sense in which he cannot choose his religion either. It is not possible to bring up children in this country *as though* Christianity had not been the religion of Europe for centuries, soaked into our language and customs. Conversely, although anybody can become personally convinced of the truth and cogency of Buddhism as a faith and can join a Buddhist society in many cities of the West, yet he cannot become the sort of Buddhist who has been formed by a totality of Buddhist culture, with all the unspoken assumptions that go with being from birth surrounded by its sights and sounds, speaking a language in which all its terms are at home, in a community whose basic values are largely formed by it.

As any convert really allows himself to be taken over by the outlook of his new religion so he learns the truth of a comment by Hendrik Kraemer.[1] 'It constitutes one of the most formidable things that can happen to an individual or a group: to start to grow with an entirely different spiritual orientation in an old and well known environment.' This traumatic experience does not belong to growing up in a religious culture. What the convert first becomes is not the inheritor of a religious culture, but a believer, an adherent in my second sense. He 'joins', probably by having met articulate believers and exponents of the new faith in person or through books, and only slowly do the new roots grow. Bringing up his children in the new faith is an important part of his own experience: but the children themselves sometimes feel a sense of loss, either that they are removed from the surrounding religious culture, or that they personally cannot have what was obviously an experience of such overwhelming importance to their parents.

The same experience is shared by whole groups of people changing their faith: a village for example. Their will and intention is towards the change (conversion means in Greek change of direction), times of crisis will tempt them back to older cultural practices: then the new faith is on trial but, when the crises are over, reliance on the new faith and the

[1] HENDRIK KRAEMER, *Religion and the Christian Faith* (Lutterworth, 1958), p. 388.

practices that go with it increases. For anyone who marries across the boundaries of religious culture, the most difficult things to grow accustomed to are those the other partner takes for granted without conscious commitment. Even those whose education and outlook have been secularized may find that the birth of children or the death of parents are events likely to reveal different assumptions: a deeply inbred knowledge of how to feel and act in the presence of birth or death may suddenly conflict with what the mind thinks and with opinions expressed.

What will be the future of religion as the cultural bond expressed in acts and attitudes common to large numbers of people? In the past these have often shown themselves peculiarly resistant to outside attack, surviving secretly long periods of persecution or the imposition of other cultural forms overlaying them. But will religion in this sense die away with the spread of urbanization, industrialization, a scientific outlook, universal education and all the 'acids of modernity' of which the distinguished Roman Catholic layman Friedrich von Hügel wrote many years ago? Or will it in fact prove to be the most lasting part of religion?

This is a question that particularly affects the professionals of religion. They are the ones who in most religions perform the rites and ceremonies of the cultus: doing so may occupy a considerable part of their time. In a society already largely secularized, on what assumptions about the future ought they to act: on the assumption that religion is an essential ingredient of life and that they are therefore in some sense trustees for a future which will rediscover this: or on the assumption that the future of religion is in minority groups formed of those who want to belong? On the latter assumption their concern should be with the minority and with the majority only in their capacity as citizens. A third possible course is that they keep an open mind about both possibilities. This means accusations of performing neither function to everybody's satisfaction, while espousing one course to the exclusion of the other – were that in all cases legally and practically possible – would mean attempting to decide the future in the present state of great fluidity.

Those opposing points of view are embattled within Christianity at present. Although they press upon the professionals in different ways in state churches or national churches on the one hand and in free churches on the other, the basic situation is the same. Although there is no established church in the United States, the problem of the committed religious minority and the majority to whom religion is part of the American way of life, is a version of the same thing. Other religions also have opposite or contending drives towards the future. Buddhist nationalism and Buddhist missionary expansionism are not based on identical assumptions about society or religion's cultural role.

The Social Aspects of Religious Rites

The future of the religious cultus has social and even political aspects to it. The same ceremonies that to the individual believer have a religious authority perform and always have performed a social role: they are unitive and stabilizing in society. Many people think of religion not as something they would want to join or belong to but as a way of signifying the importance of an event by doing what is traditional, dignified and acceptable. Any state, and not least the welfare state, sees advantages in stable marriages, and marriage laws are a social necessity if the law is ever likely to have to protect either party or their children. Church and state agree, as the notices in registry offices make clear, that in this country marriage is entered upon as the enduring partnership of one man with one woman.

Other rites are important as both religious and social

ceremonies. Baptism brings the family together for the public naming of the child and stresses the personal responsibility of parents and sponsors for him. The rites of burial which religiously interpret the transitoriness of life and the hope beyond it, turn the disposal of a body into the act of 'committal', as the Book of Common Prayer calls it. It is important that birth and death should be *namings* and *somebody's* death and that the community should have better ways of doing honour to persons than reporting their names for the registrar's records. Where religion fades or is discouraged there still seems to be a need to dignify 'rites of passage' and socialist countries from time to time take action to try to do this because of the tendency to return to the church for something the state does not provide. Recent Soviet cartoons have ridiculed party members for having their children baptized. Many humanists admit that thus far they have not found ways of dignifying the main events of personal life with ceremonies that provide an adequate substitute for religious ceremonies. It may be that it is precisely the outreach of religion beyond what the humanist regards as the given confines of human life that provides what people sense that they need; for birth and death are not incidents in a life: in them a life touches its strange boundary between being and non-being.

There are many other rites than those associated with birth, marriage and death. Coronation is too obvious a one to need stressing, except perhaps to point out that the greater participation in the coronation of Queen Elizabeth II by a mass audience through television had the effect of enhancing rather than diminishing its dignity and its significance as a national rite. Accounts of the coronations of Queen Victoria and her predecessors show a degree of ineptitude by some of the main ecclesiastical professionals, and a disorderliness among the peers present, that added up to anything but a solemn religious occasion. Archbishop Fisher's annotated copy of the service book used at the coronation of Queen Elizabeth II (to be seen in the library of Lambeth Palace) details every action of the Queen and all the participants and shows a combination of high professionalism with a personal concern for participants acting under the gaze of millions of eyes. The emotion is what the public brought to it, and this underlines a function of all the Christian rites under discussion, that it is not the business of the professionals to engender emotion but to provide a means for the emotion that is felt by the participants concerning what the rite is about to discharge itself. That statement however should not be understood as a generalization about all religious rites in any religion. They have many purposes and a large literature on their function has explored them and theorized about them.

New rites and ceremonies come into being to express human needs. Independence days are mainly secular occasions on which there may or may not be religious services. The Jewish (Israeli) day of independence is an interesting case, for it is developing a religious form in which the reading of the Messianic prophecies and prayers of thanksgiving and memorial of victims of Nazi atrocities take a place.

Harvest festivals began only after England had become a mainly industrial country. Memorial services have accompanied the growth of the practice of cremation and the difficulty of summoning people at short notice to funerals in inaccessible places. One could lengthen the list of ceremonies that affect parts of a population, but the real function of a religious cultus is that its rites affect all at some period of their lives or have to do with national representative occasions like a coronation or a state funeral.

A conspicuous lack in Christianity is any rite that celebrates puberty and the beginnings of sexual activity. Primitive societies do this by initiation ceremonies which mark the beginning of adulthood. Hinduism is totally uninhibited in its relating of sex to religion: fertility as the source of life, is honoured. The New Testament by contrast develops religious insight into the meaning of married love. The unity of the couple as one flesh, the mutuality of love and caring which are enjoined upon them and above all the strict emphasis on monogamy enhanced the position of the woman in marriage as compared with the surrounding world. Potentially the New Testament made the status of woman in marriage that of a person in her own right instead of the agent of a man's relationship with his sons. The love of Christ for his church in giving himself for it is enjoined on husbands by the New Testament as the example to follow in their relation to their wives.

But Christianity has not been able to come to terms with the fire and passion of sexual love and so to celebrate its awakening as the gift of a good creator. The doctrine of original sin, which is not found in the Old Testament or in the gospels, was developed by St. Augustine from St. Paul and threw a long shadow over the Christian understanding of human sexuality. The sex act was barely redeemed by its procreative aspects and never by its unitive. Christianity has come in for much just criticism. But on the other hand it must be said that the religions which have venerated sexuality and stress it are not the ones that have uplifted women: it is woman's fertility not her sexuality which is usually the object of such veneration.

So now, unable any longer to exert over youth the controls of a former age, the church has left open the way for a complete secularization of the celebration of sexual love. In the songs of the pop singers one sees glimpses of what might have been a part of the religious cultus, which was indeed present always in folk song and dance but never recognized by the church or given formal means of expression. But there is also present in the pop music of today the inability to transcend the cramped expression of appetite passing into possession and back again to appetite. True initiation opens the door to maturity. The celebration of perpetual adolescence expresses the fear, not the confidence, of joining the adult world, and that fear in modern society may be justified.

*

The reasons for the continuance of the religious cultus into what is or is always called a secular age would take a great deal of analysis. Nobody can refer to marriage in church as a 'relic' of the religious past when the numbers of such marriages involve in this country seven hundred of every thousand of the marriages that take place. No other religion but Christianity and no other age but this has measured religious performance by the regularity of attendance at weekly services. To suggest that English people who are not good at measuring up to this yardstick are in fact more religious than the secularists hope and the religious fear is to court the criticism of unrealism: one is accused of just not facing facts: the question is what facts? The constant suggestion that people take part in these rites 'without understanding their full implications' prompts the question whether all of them ever did? It is of the nature of rites to be meaningful to all levels of intelligence and not to be replaceable by verbalizations on their meaning comprehensible only to theologians. When one considers that now there is more general education and more open discussion of questions of belief and conformity than ever before, and that people are not under the ecclesiastical and social pressures – sanctions would not be much too strong a word – that prevailed a hundred years ago, is there not at least the likelihood that people conform less by comparison than they did and engage in these rites because they want to?

The self-questioning of the professionals, or at least of some

of them, forms part of the debate about the future of the
cultus. Most of them welcome every opportunity of making
contact with people, helping them to bring something to the
rite that is their own, and to take from it a strength. But many
of them occasionally and some of them somewhat vocifer-
ously (in the columns of the religious press) raise the question
whether people are led in these rites to say things they do not
understand and undertake promises they either do not intend
to keep or do not understand as promises. In one sense the
professionals are best placed to answer their own questions
from the interviews that they have with a considerable
proportion of partners intending to marry, parents of children
brought for baptism and relatives of the dead. This is far more
common than it used to be because, contrary perhaps to some
opinions, the professionals in any even moderately heavily
populated area work far harder than their predecessors and
quite as hard as most other professionals.

The questions raised above centre mainly on baptism. It is
one of the two chief sacraments of the Christian Church and
is the rite of admission to it. In the form in which it is adminis-
tered in the Church of England it demands both a confession
of faith on the part of the sponsors and promises made by
them on behalf of the child. Adherents in the second sense
of the word will want baptism for their children: they will
count themselves as believers and be prepared to accept the
responsibilities. Outside that stricter definition there will be
many who will not count themselves as adherents in the sense
of churchgoers but who would want to behave as they think
a Christian should in the conduct of their lives and to bring
up their children in that sort of way. But the professional
knows quite well that there are yet others who bring the
child for baptism in a different spirit: the grandmother wants
it; the parents do not want to leave anything undone for the
child that might be, however marginally, an advantage; or

how else would one justify the celebration afterwards if one did not have the christening? While a few clergy protest that the practice of baptism should be discouraged among any but those who are professing Christians, the majority think that the proper course is to reform the rite and make its meaning clearer rather than to discourage those who come. This would enable people to include or exclude themselves by their own decision. Some churches already provide an alternative in the naming and blessing of children in church. I suspect that a great many people think of baptism as this in any case and that it could become an acceptable alternative rite. The fewer professionals there are in proportion to a population the lower the proportion of people taking part in the rites of religion. This is made clear in Mr. Leslie Paul's study *The Deployment and Payment of the Clergy*[1] and in the official statistics of the Church of England.[2] A cast-iron proof of a causal connection cannot be shown but the statistics bear out what one would suspect, for the rites and ceremonies of the church cannot go on without the professionals, who must be accessible. As *they* decline in numbers, so will the availability of these rites to the population at large. Every baptism, marriage, burial is an individual ceremony. Somebody has to take an initiative towards the professionals before any one of them can be performed. It seems to me remarkable that there are so many.

*

How, if at all, do those who join in the rites and ceremonies

[1] See footnote, p. 52.
[2] *Statistics of the Church of England*, published every second year by the Church Information Office. A mine of information, with comparisons with the past.

The *World Christian Handbook*, edited by Sir KENNETH GRUBB for the Survey Application Trust, published by Lutterworth Press, gives world-wide figures for all churches.

of religion come to know anything about its teaching and the claims it makes on practice, both religious and moral?

The answer in the case of some religions is that the performance of the rites is almost if not quite the whole content of the religion. This would be true of any nature worship or naturalistic religion.

Hinduism has no rite of entry except birth, and birth is in itself a sign of one's status within the organization of the religion. Duty is to carry out what is proper according to one's birth, for birth within one caste or another or as man or woman is decided not by chance but by one's previous life achievement. The father teaches his son, the mother her daughter. No one but the Brahman is expected to study the scriptures or to carry out duties other than attendance at the rites, though others do, and there are general precepts or traditions of behaviour – not to show anger, for example, and duties relating to one's sex and station.

In Buddhism the essential heart of the religion is in personal following of the eightfold path, therefore a form of self education and self-discipline is required. But popular Buddhism has developed rites including the making of offerings at shrines, the burning of incense, often before the statue of the Buddha and the saying of prayers and repetition of formularies. Both Hinduism and Buddhism in their popular forms are accompanied by a strong belief in charms, luck and especially astrology. Hinduism has always been a social system with its basis in caste. Through caste the duties of religion were performed. The state of India has legislated against discrimination on grounds of caste in public service, the law, entry to temples and education. But caste is almost always observed in the choice of marriage partners. Hindu marriage (which takes place in the home) is preserved even in families that have departed from the practice of devotion to the gods; and the search for the right bride or groom is

pursued both with the aid of horoscopes and in the advertise-
ment columns of the newspapers.

In Judaism the cultus is carried on partly in the home and
partly in the synagogue. Birth of a Jewish *mother* is the rite
of entry into Judaism and is regarded by Jews as irreversible
even by conversion to another faith. The rite of circumcision
of males on the eighth day after birth, in the home, and by a
Jewish rabbi or doctor is not the rite of admission except for
proselytes (converts). The father or head of the family is
responsible for the instruction of the young in the Torah.
At thirteen the boy goes to the synagogue and is ready to
take his turn in the reading of the Torah there. The chief of
the three great feasts, the Passover, is celebrated in the home
and in the rich symbolism of the rehearsal of the flight from
Egypt which made the Jews a nation even the youngest child
has his part to play. Marriage also takes place in the home.
Even non-religious Jews take part in some of the festivals
such as the Jewish New Year which celebrates the Creation
and is a time of public rejoicing. In spite of the growth around
the synagogue of activities including teaching and works of
charity in modern Judaism, the continuance of the religion
in the home is the real means by which religion is taught and
its obligations met.

In Christianity those who belong in the sense of still taking
part in the religious cultus have two main ways of keeping
in touch with the teaching and practice of religion. The first
is by going to church occasionally, the second is by being
taught in school. Probably about forty per cent of English
people (possibly more) attend church occasionally, varying
from once or twice a week to three times a year. The most
popular special occasions are Christmas, Easter and harvest
festival, but occasional attendance at ordinary services also
takes place. The figures given emerge from the national
opinion polls and from inquiries made in connection with

religious broadcasting, which is another means by which a large minority, especially of the middle aged, keep in touch with religion. Churchgoing is much higher among Roman Catholics than among other adherents. Sunday schools are declining in numbers: youth organizations provide some contact with churches for a minority of the age group.

There is no doubt that the main source of contact with the teaching and practice of religion is for most people in this country the second: through the schools. While the professionals of Christianity are the ones who carry on the cultus 'the main teacher of religion in this country is a lady in a primary school'.[1] In fact the schools are the only contact that many boys and girls have with religion.

Before turning to the provision that is made here a brief glance at what happens elsewhere and in relation to other religions may be useful.

Most countries of the world (except communist countries) make provision for the teaching of religion in schools. The ways in which this is done are extremely varied, and the details are summarized country by country by Unesco in its World Surveys of primary education (1958) and secondary education (1961).

Outside Europe the teaching of the predominant religion is the chief provision and usually this is done by the religious professionals rather than by the teachers. Where there is a mixture of religions sometimes the state supports financially schools organized on a religious basis; or the teaching of religion to the children of adherents by the professionals of that faith is allowed on school premises in school time. In many parts of Asia, in the Pacific, in most of Africa south of the Sahara and in many countries of Latin America, a very high proportion of the schools are run by Christian churches,

[1] DAVID MARTIN, *A Sociology of English Religion* (S.C.M., 1967) pp. 88–9.

missions or religious orders, increasingly with government support. The independent nations that have emerged in the last twenty years have come to different arrangements with religious bodies: in some cases the schools have been taken over, but in very many the governments are dependent on the contribution made by these schools as they try to create a national system of education with slender means. In some countries (Egypt for example) schools under Christian auspices must teach the main religion (Islam). Where a substantial proportion of the population is Christian, Christian teaching continues in the schools even if taken over by government and provision for minorities is made as needed, enforced by law or regulation. In some cases the effect of national policies in education has been to shake the teaching out of its westernized form. In Western Europe nearly all countries with the exception of France have religious teaching in the school. In mainly Roman Catholic countries the teaching is usually done by members of the religious orders but in other countries (including an Orthodox country like Greece) the teaching is done by the regular teachers.

Religious education in state schools or in voluntary schools receiving some state support is therefore very far from a rarity, and where the opinion of parents or of the public is sought it seems to favour its continuance. The national opinion polls and the Institute of Education of the University of Newcastle have both carried out investigation into the percentage of parents in an adequate sample who want their children to receive religious instruction in state day schools. The answer in both cases was ninety per cent. When the Swedish government in 1962 introduced a new system of secondary education and proposed to omit religious instruction from one of the new types of schools the resultant expression of public opinion was in the same proportions.

Against this solidarity of opinion in favour must be put

the opposing opinions in the United States and in France. From the earliest days the American constitution has contained an article separating church and state. There is therefore no established church. Every religion has equal rights and none have access to the public schools for purposes of religious instruction. Religious education is carried on in some cases in what is called 'release time' at the end of the school day, and on church premises by professional and voluntary religious educators. American churches spend (by any other standards) vast sums on this enterprise. It had gradually become the custom, however, in many schools to say what was called 'the regents' prayer', i.e. a prayer authorized by the governing boards. A single parent by challenging this in one court precipitated Supreme Court decisions which interpreted the constitution as prohibiting first the saying of prayers of any kind and then all teaching of any religious scriptures. Nearly all church leaders welcomed the Supreme Court's ruling as right in itself and consistent with their jealously guarded position under the constitution. But it was later realized that strictly interpreted the ruling would forbid reference in schools to the scriptures or the practices of any religion in the teaching of literature, history or any other subject.

Religion is more widely accepted as a part of education than many people think. But there is a great deal of questioning in many countries about its future role: the issue is not the same everywhere but varies from one culture to another. In this country the difficulties felt today are usually thought to have their focus in the unsatisfactory nature of the religious clauses of the 1944 Education Act and the way they have worked out in practice. Possibly however it would be nearer the facts of the situation to say that the Act was very successful in one respect – that of ending the disgraceful and damaging disputes of religious bodies – but at the price of imposing a rigidity that has prevented educational criteria from having the priority they should have had in relation to religious education. Our problem is not an Act of Parliament, nor was it created by any Act: it is the far more fundamental one of the place of religious education and what that very phrase means in the kind of society and the kind of education that we have today – so radically different from the England and the 'National' and 'British' Schools in which the lady in a primary school began her career in the early years of last century.

It may have advantages to turn away from the problem of schools to the relation of religion to education in areas where the writ of the 1944 Act does not run, that is in higher education and further education.

The universities are marked by their own histories. Oxford and Cambridge colleges were first Catholic and then Anglican foundations, and their chapels were the focus of their religious life. But in the highly diversified college communities of today Christians (at least in the sense of any active profession) are a small minority, of whom many will find their place of religious attachment in a local church rather than a college chapel. But like much else in a university the fortunes of college chapels ebb and flow and some will, for a time at any rate, have lively congregations. A small number of colleges carry on their musical tradition – King's College, Cambridge, and Magdalen College, Oxford, are the most famous, with their choirs and choir schools, but others with fewer resources still keep a musical tradition in being. (When these colleges, and the choir schools of the cathedrals, go under to the march of educational progress someone will perhaps regret that the most famous musical tradition in England and the only one that was ever the envy of continentals has died and that all English music suffers from their loss: education too will be the poorer from the loss of this distinctive small strand within it: but this is a tempting digression.)

Oxford and Cambridge colleges are still communities, but not religious communities. Many in them would agree that religion suffers from the identification with 'establishment' which for the majority of young people is a shorthand term for what they most dislike. But there is no lack of the discussion of religious ideas, in which the formal figures associated with religion play their part in accordance with their ability to communicate through or in spite of the traditional forms of religion that they are committed to uphold. The role of the chaplain differs: the Oxford chaplain is typically a teaching fellow of his college, while the typical Cambridge chaplain is not much older than the undergraduates and is unlikely to have teaching responsibilities.

In the civic universities, the department, especially if it is a small one, is something of a community, but is based on work rather than residence. The older civic universities were non-residential and religion was not part of their establishment – indeed some of them were founded precisely in order to be free of the restrictions that religious establishment placed on the older universities. As their students were almost all local there was no thought of providing either chapels or chaplains. All universities are now national institutions drawing their students from far and wide, including nearly ten per cent from overseas, and halls of residence and lodgings meet the need for accommodation. Religious needs used to be met by local churches and by voluntary societies among students until some twenty-five years ago, when denominational chaplains began to be appointed by church authorities, first as part-timers, later (at least in the case of Anglicans and Roman Catholics) as full-timers. The first intention of the church authorities was that chaplains should shepherd their own denominational flocks, but for chaplains themselves the challenge of the university, which is so seldom a community, has seemed to call for something more both in terms of the relations between Christians and in terms of making religious worship and activity really minister to a largely migrant community constantly passing through academic life.

Another aspect of religion in the university is the teaching of theology there. Oxford made theology an examinable subject in 1870 and only after much debate. The object was to give to those who were to become clergymen of the Church of England a more thorough grounding in the scriptures. All sorts of fears were expressed for the future: on the one hand that the teaching might become too secular, on the other that it might be too much dominated by concern about the orthodoxy or otherwise of the examinees or even the examiners to take its place alongside other disciplines. The situation was a difficult one, for there were those on both sides of the debate who looked back to the time when in the medieval university theology had been 'the queen of the sciences'. In both the older universities as in those of Scotland also, the overwhelming majority of students of theology were intending to enter the ministry of a church. But the pressure of the university was always towards introducing emphases that stressed the comparability of theology with other studies in objectivity of method and in content. Thus not systematic theology but the history of doctrine was taught; the main content continued to be the Bible assuming a knowledge of at least Greek and often Hebrew and adding to it such academically respectable aids as textual criticism and archeology. Nothing contemporary appeared, and nothing of recent history. Reform has been far from easy: to add fresh content meant that something had to be omitted. But to re-define the aims was and is even more difficult: ought theology to become so estranged from the gusto that characterizes living faith that it provides no essential spark of religious imagination? Does it fully serve either the believer who wants to add religious learning to faith, or the unbeliever who would like to know by the engagement of theology within the university where he is learning something else, what it is supposed to be about?

The civic universities were in some cases banned by their charters from setting up theological faculties at all: others could do so only in such terms as the *history* of religion. But in some there were larger possibilities and new departments of theology were established and began to grow. Their range covered such subjects as recent church history in a world perspective, ethics, liturgy and modern problems of Biblical interpretation based upon a philosophical understanding of language. Among their students were and are many with no intention of being ordained, many women, some intending to be teachers and others expecting to find a pastoral vocation in the social services or industry. Theology as a possible form of liberal education rather than vocational education appeared in the modern universities.

A further step has been taken in some of the new universities and new departments established since the war: this is the attempt to work out courses in religious studies which either broaden the scope of a theology department to include the study of other religions and of ethical philosophies or, from a small base of theologically trained teachers, create for the students courses in religious studies options which draw also on the services of historians, psychologists, sociologists and others.

In many colleges of education religious studies can be offered as the major subject of a three-year course, along with education as a professional course. It can also be taken in the Bachelor of Education degree in most of the university institutes of education. In the colleges, as in the universities, there have been marked changes. The change in emphasis is from learning to teach a subject to studying for the sake of the intellectual and personal development and maturity of the student, without which training is of little avail. Religious studies have been particularly affected by this change. The general expectancy was until a few years ago that nearly all primary school teachers would teach religious knowledge to children: the specialist was almost unknown. Religion seemed to be passed by in the trend towards an abolition of 'subject teaching' in the primary school and religious education was the last subject to take account of modern knowledge of the development of thought and emotions in young children. Within many colleges there are now longer and more thorough courses for students making religious studies their academic study, ranging in different colleges from the study of worship to the psychology of religion, from biblical history to ethics. Gone are the days when teachers only learned to tell Bible stories and children were regarded as empty pitchers to be filled.

In further education, both part-time and full-time, there is an opportunity for the study of religion as a part of courses in liberal studies. For the resourceful teacher, further education offers a stimulating field in which to work. Colleges of further education can usually supply courses in religious subjects when they are demanded and such courses form a part of a wide range of courses for adults. Closely parallel to this, sometimes within further education colleges, sometimes in extra-mural centres of universities, are the courses for adults that lead to a qualification. There are more part-time students working for degrees and diplomas in theology externally than there are students of theology in all the universities. Many are teachers with a qualification in another subject. One further point needs to be made. Many of the subjects that are taught in universities and colleges do in fact raise religious issues which those who teach them are not necessarily able or willing to discuss. The presence of theological teaching means the presence of books on theological topics in the library and persons on the teaching staff whose knowledge may be useful. It also means that students who want them have the chance of courses and discussions outside or on the margins of their own specialism.

All that has thus far been discussed of religious education is concerned with people over school-leaving age and outside the framework of the 1944 Act. Very little of it is directly influenced by the actions of the churches: there are church colleges of education (Anglican, Catholic and Methodist) but no Catholic or other church universities (as there are in many parts of the world) or institutions of further education. How therefore does what goes on in these sectors of education have any bearing on what happens in the schools?

First, it is this sector of education that provides the teachers for the schools: any changes here whether of the content of theology and religious studies or in the mood and approach of teachers and students will shortly be reflected in the schools. Secondly, a good deal of the articulate criticism of religious education in the schools, including the best informed part of it, comes from the schools themselves, from teachers and students in higher education and from an articulate and educated minority among parents. Thirdly, a very considerable amount of research has now been done (more is to come) on many aspects of religious education and has made many older views of it inapplicable. This research emanates from universities and from colleges of education. Such research has been influential not only in the colleges and schools but in the churches also. Much of it is applicable to their own teaching programmes and processes and all of it is highly relevant to the work of the agreed syllabus committees on which, in accordance with the provisions of the Act, church representatives sit with teachers to prepare the syllabuses which, legally speaking, are the basis of religious education in our schools. A distinguished churchman and educator, the

Roman Catholic Archbishop of Liverpool acknowledged the importance of one piece of such research thus:

> Modern educational methods are strongly child-centred in subjects such as number, language and science. It may be a matter for surprise that we have had to wait so long to see developmental assessments applied to religious teaching, yet what are now called the pre-religious, sub-religious and the personal religious stages in the development of a child are, in most cases, clearly discernible and each stage calls for its characteristic teaching. This may be summed up by saying that the teaching must correspond to the growing experience of the child and that enrichment of that experience even at the natural level is an important aspect of religious education.[1]

There are three parties to the religious and moral education of the child – the family (especially the parents), the school (especially the teachers, but also the peer group of each particular child) and the church (directly in relation to some children through Sunday school, club, youth organization, and indirectly through the training of teachers and the forming of agreed syllabuses). There is strong ground for saying that the foundations of a child's moral education are laid before he ever comes under the direct influence of a teacher: the same would be true of his religious education in the sense that a secure and happy home is the best foundation of spiritual growth. Recent educational research[2] has shown that the influence of parents on the educational development of their children grows rather than diminishes as the child passes through the primary school. No teacher can hope to reverse or correct the continuous influence of the home: and

[1] The Most Revd. G. A. Beck, Archbishop of Liverpool, in *Looking forward to the Seventies* (Colin Smyth, 1968).

[2] Summarized in *Children and their primary Schools* (the Plowden Report) (H.M.S.O.).

if the teacher is going to reinforce the best in the home and the local culture, she needs to know more about it.

The 1944 Education Act never envisaged that the schools could do more than make *a contribution* to the spiritual and moral education of children. Two disasters have overtaken that contribution: one the expectation of many parents that all that was needed the school could do, the other the failure of the relevant authorities to provide adequately for the contribution the schools were to make, by remedying the drastic shortfall of specialist teachers and by providing enough opportunities for teachers in service to equip themselves better for the task. More has had to be attempted with less resource. Unless the parents play their part neither religious nor moral education separately or together can be effective in the schools. But it is idle just to condemn parents: they need help. Many are thoroughly puzzled both about religion and about what is the right and the good. Life in industrial England does not present clearcut issues of right and wrong or uncomplicated loyalties, any more than it presses in with intimations of a divine order. A society which continuously advertises, as supreme satisfactions in life, possessions and entertainment cannot blame parents for accepting and passing on the message. Certainly there are signs among young people today that goals of this kind do not satisfy: for some, disgust begets an escape to fantasy either in the world of the drop-out or that of the agitator without aims beyond agitation: for others, dissatisfaction leads to the search for a new dimension of responsible life. There is no evidence that the present generation of young people will make more irresponsible parents than the generation before them. They are in possession of better methods of ensuring that parenthood is deliberately chosen than any previous generation has been: they are the first generation whose educated élites are not solidly middle-class: they are capable of making a genuine cultural change. What evidence is there that religion might play any part in this? Edwin Cox's[1] *Sixth Form Religion*, published in 1968, showed the attitudes of a representative sample of sixth-formers to religion and the teaching of it that they had experienced. More than half thought religion was an important matter and that it ought to have its place in education but only a tiny minority thought that they themselves or the cause of religion had been helped by what they had encountered of it in their own schools or in the churches with which a minority had contact. For this educated minority religion is or could be important to them as persons, but the institutionalized forms of it are inadequate. Of the vast majority whose schooling ends at or shortly after the school-leaving age it is more difficult to say anything. Institutionalized Youth Service, whether local authority or voluntary body, touches only thirty per cent of the age group. Many have tried and abandoned it. The experience of the Youth Service especially in the years of effort to improve it since the Albemarle report of 1960 shows very clearly the antipathy of young people to organizational 'belonging': they want to be customers buying services, not members paying subscriptions. But this said, it also must be added that the fact of belonging means a great deal to some of that thirty per cent, and K. E. Hyde[2] has shown how religious learning (whose source is in interest) is stimulated by belonging – even by marginal belonging. On the other hand the Y.W.C.A., one of the oldest youth organizations, has shown by research and experiment the need and possibilities for work by organizationally unattached leaders among 'unattached youth' that is those who have never found supporting or lasting relation-

[1] EDWIN COX, *Sixth Form Religion* (S.C.M., 1968).
[2] K. E. HYDE, *Religious Learning in Adolescence* (University of Birmingham Press, 1965). GOETSCHIUS and TASH, *Working with Unattached Youth* (Routledge & Kegan Paul, 1967).

ships in life. These too may be among the parents of tomorrow, but they were never reached in their schools by any adult who showed the kind of caring that could get across to them.

David Martin's 'lady in a primary school', when she was as he says 'the main teacher of religion' had the support of a tremendous and recognized authority. R. C. K. Ensor says in his *England 1870–1914* that among civilized as distinct from primitive people the Victorians were one of the most religious the world has ever seen. Not only did the church play a large role in public affairs: far more important, the Bible was deeply respected by the overwhelming majority of the nation. In the school the main content of teaching was the Bible, supplemented in the schools of the Church of England and the Roman Catholics, by the teaching of their catechisms, which were usually learned by heart, as was almost everything else in education. Children were not badly served who had echoes of the Bible in their speech and its teachings as their example and the homely language of the catechism as moral precept, 'to keep my hands from picking and stealing, and my tongue from evil-speaking, lying and slandering'. The social order it presupposed has gone, so has the ecclesiastical authority that had power to command: any suspicion that it might still be trying to do so meets with instant attack. The churches therefore have to disabuse those who think that their interest in religious education in the schools is an attempt to reassert their power. They can perhaps best do this by recognizing that the teacher of religious education is not the long arm of the church but a part of the teaching body and as such concerned with the education of children. The kind of support the teacher needs today is not that of being under authority (what he has to do and say all cut and dried) but of being a free person, constantly learning in the religious field – not an authority on behalf of the church nor a substitute for the parents, and never a conscript.

As the emphasis shifts in education from teachers teaching to learners learning (though this emphasis is not new – St. Augustine vigorously supported it in the fourth century), so changes must follow in religious education. The first spiritual and moral need of the child is for a school community where he is cared for as an individual, helped to live with his fellows and free to ask his questions. Teachers of all religious views and none can help to make such a community. At the primary age the child is learning skills: religion has its skills and its basic knowledge. Some of these are important for cultural reasons and are part of every child's inheritance who shares life in this country: to know the Lord's Prayer for example and a small store of psalms and hymns, who Jesus was and some of what he said and did, the Christian law of love of God and neighbour. Worship and religious actions cannot be talked about without being exemplified in the school, as the joint humanist and Christian signatories of a recent statement recognized. The child's own growth and need dictates the pace of teaching. Anxiety to press on the child everything for fear he should never meet it elsewhere is self-defeating and can be damaging.

There is no doubt that when there is a new Education Act the question of religious education and especially the compulsory provisions of the 1944 Act will be attacked. They are ripe for revision, but not for abolition. The Act made a national framework within which local authorities and schools should operate. It needs change. If as I have argued religious education in country schools is part of the cultus and not an extension of societal belonging from churches to schools then it must change and develop to meet the needs of a society which contains on the one hand a majority having connections with traditional religion and on the other a plurality of religious and non-religious customs and beliefs.

The case for a changed religious education cannot simply be written off. People think, in an age of the non-practice of religion, that religion is important to know about, and even to do something about privately. Under the tip of the iceberg lies the unseen mass of personal choices and sentiments, the questions about man's life that have helped to make the European tradition and that keep people as 'adherents' in the cultural sense when they have long since given up, if they ever had, any commitment as members of religious societies.

The Societal Meaning of Adherence

All over Europe church leaders deplore and observers comment on the weak content of faith and knowledge which, as far as the outward eye can tell, accompanies the continued practice of the rites of religion. From what source would one expect renewal? The most obvious answer would be 'from the congregations of regular churchgoers who use the buildings that others only occasionally visit'. In what sort of shape are they for responding to such a challenge?

As one travels, reads or looks at television it is impossible not to be struck by the great antiquity of most human settlements. There seems to be a built-in trust of the wisdom of the original inhabitants in their choice of a site. Abandonment usually meant the exhaustion of natural resources more by man's misuse than nature's failure. Family, work and neighbourhood provided the context of men's lives, all in the same place. Religion bound them together and perhaps created the first leisure with its holy days and seasons. *Religion as cultural and as societal belonging were one.* So static a state of affairs can be over-drawn. Simple forms of trade, the exaction by rulers of military and other service, the wanderings of nomads and migrants in flight from wars or retribution, or seeking new homes, all break up the picture of the static local community.

Religion too made its contribution to movement and change. Pilgrimages were like an early form of tourism, and pilgrims brought home with them not only merit or holiness but new foods, materials, ideas and diseases, opening up the static community to the wider world. This has to be said because of the tendency to look upon former ages as times in which religion was nothing but the local community with its religious building in the middle saying 'come' to the local inhabitants. The village received its visitants even if rarely. The East has had an age-old tradition of holy men and sages spending their lives in moving from place to place, many doing no more than receive charity, but some bringing some new message or practice. Medieval Europe also had many such travellers.

I have already described (Chapter II) how in Western Europe the religious building became the place of meeting for congregations gathering together out of the general community, till now 'church' means the place where such people gather, the people, and their wider connections through denominational and ecumenical bodies with others.

At present there is among many people a mood bordering on despair about the *local* church. The old say it used to be different, the young say it ought to be. One of the factors in this mood is that of living in the shadow of an era of great achievement in local congregations. A visit to eighteenth-century English church life would not encourage: ultra-conservative bishops, many idle clergy dependent on the squirearchy, worldly congregations in the established churches and in dissenting ones, much social indifference and intellectual scepticism. Yet in the eighteenth century were sown the seeds of the astonishing revival of the life of local congregations in the nineteenth.

The origins of Methodism are obscure, but the practice of group disciplines of prayer and devotion long preceded the

Wesleys. Their preaching led to societal belonging in groups under lay leaders: still the basic form of Methodism. The evangelical revival which reached such proportions in the nineteenth century had its origins in the recovery of personal piety in the eighteenth. It affected every protestant country in Europe and every church. In England groups of distinguished men like the Clapham Sect working for the abolition of slavery finally achieved not only that end but the beginning of changes of attitude among many churchmen. In every country there was some different social manifestation of a new personal religious energy. In Denmark it was the folk high schools, a model for adult education. In Germany it was the 'Inner Mission' founded in the years of famine and near-chaos which followed the Napoleonic wars. Immanuel Wichern of Hamburg and his wife took into their home boys turned into beggars and criminals by the terrible conditions of their childhood. Encouraged by the success of the Rough House, Wichern trained other young men and soon there were twenty training workshops and farms with their homes for the boys. This brotherhood of dedicated men went on to other tasks, and as their social work widened its range so volunteers from local congregations began to take a part. A little later a German pastor named Fliedner founded at Kaiserswerth a house for nursing the sick poor in which he and a physician colleague trained seven women as deaconesses, that is with the complementary skills of nursing and pastoral care. With astonishing speed the requests for training came and Fliedner within a few years had given Miss Nightingale her training and had also established groups of deaconesses in Egypt and in North America. Organized by 'mother houses' the deaconesses worked in hospitals and as parish nurses in almost every European country and many other parts of the world. Again, the presence of these new professionals gave an outlet for service and provided the means for

voluntary support and assistance to rally. The parish deaconesses were often very successful in cities where traditional
preaching methods were failing to communicate.

A third movement of equal power in reviving the congregations was the establishment of missions for work overseas.
These also began in the eighteenth century and exerted their
greatest influence on church life in the nineteenth and early
twentieth centuries. The motives of foreign missionary work
broadened from the early conceptions of preaching to a large
operation of medical, educational, social and agricultural
work. The extent of their work is still surprisingly large: for
example the American Mission boards at present send a hundred million dollars a year overseas in support of their work:
the highest item of expenditure is education in colleges,
schools and training institutions of many kinds. The foreign
missionary movement, in spite of its many weaknesses of
outlook, had a broadening effect on the interests of congregations. It relaid for non-Catholic Christianity the foundations
of an awareness of the Church as a world-wide institution
which their efforts had been the agency of spreading to new
areas; it made the churches gradually aware of the weakening
influence of division. In America the work of foreign missions
was closely linked with work within the country – on the
expanding frontier and for the education and medical care
of the Indians.

In England the Oxford Movement revived the Catholic
life of parishes in the Church of England and brought new
colour, dignity and theological depth to worship, counter-
balancing the emotionalism and individualism of the evan-
gelicals. 'Liturgical renewal' is now a phrase to be heard in
every country in every Christian denomination. The aims
are similar – greater simplicity and clarity, and far greater
participation by lay people. New liturgies all give room for
whole congregations to be less passive and for individual

lay people to play significant parts in the public worship.

If one looks at the situation in Europe as a whole, the following three generalizations have some validity.

First, a great deal of the effort of the nineteenth and twentieth centuries has expended itself by the achievement of its goals. State social service takes the place of parish social work: the expansionist enthusiasm for missionary work has declined with the decline of the imperial expansion which it accompanied: some of the most vigorous centres of congregational life are now deserted with the change of their neighbourhood. Changes in society and in social habits have hit the local congregation and its organizations very hard indeed, in declining numbers and sense of social relevance.

Second, a smaller number of professionals in relation to the population are stretched between the claims of the society of adherents and the maintaining of the cultus. While the continental and especially the German stress is traditionally on preaching and the American on the building of community life, the English emphasis is on the pastoral ministry. Clergy and ministers may dislike being called 'professionals' and claim that they are among the few amateurs left. The divided claims of their work make professionalism in the right and good sense of that word (i.e. standards applied by corporate self-discipline) hard to achieve. Which claim ought to have priority over, and therefore shape, the other? Sometimes it is a matter of who pays. National churches usually have endowments or income from taxes for the payment of the clergy. They may be committed to providing a ministry related to areas without regard to density of population or type of need or the presence or absence of other churches. Other churches have nothing from these sources, or too little to count; in their case, although they may disguise the fact by central accounting, the local congregations pay for the professionals. 'Can you really believe', I have been asked,

'that the future of Christianity lies with local congregations?'
I do not know: how could I? But I believe it to be urgent
that many more of the professionals have their place and mode
of work related to those places and times of life where the
greatest number of people are most in need of a pastoral
ministry, for someone to help them to believe and hope and
overcome the *diminution* of their humanity that many suffer.
I believe that the rites of religion are an important part of
such a pastoral ministry.

Therefore in regard to the future of local congregations I
would say that it is a case of seeing what happens when a
radical re-deployment of the professionals and the money
takes place. Probably many will disappear: that is a calculated
risk but one to which perhaps there is no longer any real
alternative. What is essential to my mind is to see that
people – all people – are within reach of the services of the
professional ministry, if they want them, not that this or that
small group is kept in tenuous being by spreading the services
of the professionals too thin. Local congregations or groups
of congregations which have enough vision to live in an
outgoing way may well find that, in a society as educated and
as skilled as ours is, new forms of non-professional ministry
will emerge from within under the pressure of new determination. Many denominations have set their courses now
in the general direction of re-deploying their professional
ministries and diversifying them. It has yet to be proved that
they really will set the professionals free (after selection and
more thorough training) for a ministry that follows the lines
of society's development, or whether, as they have done in
the past, they will only move from one place to another the
structures of worship and corporate life that are so familiar
and, in many respects, so inadequate.

Thirdly, although many local congregations contain an
amount of heterodoxy of personal belief that might surprise

their pastors and masters, possibly there is now a new situation affecting some of them, coming from the mood of our times. It is summed up in the phrase 'God is dead', to express a feeling of doubt and uncertainty, of collapsing belief. This is a phrase with a hundred and fifty years of history in Europe, philosophical, romantic and theological. The experience it describes today, especially for a person brought up in religious faith, is as though a near relative who was away from home occasionally took to longer and longer absences and the thought began to arise 'will he perhaps not come back?' until every thought of him is of his absence and the absence takes the place of any positive statement about him. He is dead. This experience is described as 'not so much the absence of the experience of God as the experience of the absence of God'. 'It must be heard' says the head of a German radio station closely in touch with the responses of a wide selection of listeners 'not as a philosophical or theological statement but as a cry'.

It is not surprising that doubt should have this form in the Germany of Hegel and Nietzsche. In this country there is less inclination to turn emotions into slogans. Yet the reactions to Bishop Robinson's *Honest to God* showed on the one hand the relief of many that a bishop had articulated what they felt and on the other the horror that a bishop should do anything but stand against the tide of questioning. The decline of belief in life after death, even among regular churchgoers, is a sign of the weakness of the concept of transcendence. The admission made by many people that their prayers are addressed to a God not very different from the old man on a cloud that they addressed at seven shows the concept to be not only weak but static. Small wonder then that many parents are concerned about the religious education of their children, and that few churchgoers are willing or able to talk about their faith to others and, unlike the Muslim who has always spread the faith himself, regard mission as mainly an affair for specialists.

Roman Catholics always show up better in opinion polls both as to attendance and as to belief. The close identification of cultus, adherence and belief has accounted for this in the past and still does. But where this nexus is broken, as for example by education, the pressure of self-questioning arises.

Reinforcements and Alternatives: the Search for Personal Faith

It is difficult in the present scene to separate out the search for a personal faith from the search for the social meaning of faith itself. People are looking for faith and for the means of expressing it at one and the same time. Few but neurotics want an assurance that they personally are saved and the world damned: but there are those who are looking for an authentication of the faith they have been brought up in by an experience to make it their own. This is the place to mention sections of protestantism, movements in churches, some religious denominations and a number of sects – which hold that a crisis or conversion must take place in the life of an individual even if he has been brought up as a believer. In its extremer forms this belief in the need for conversion, accompanied and indeed caused by a view of man as unregenerate and liable to eternal penalties without it, produced intense suffering in some children. That conversion experience may be a cultural pattern seems to be the implication of Dr. Owen Brandon's research.[1] He found that bodies with a high expectation of conversion had a high incidence of it, but the converts come from within the same or similar groups and only rarely from groups without this expectation. One can see parallels to adolescent religious conversions in the practices of some primitive peoples. Just as an introduction to

[1] OWEN BRANDON, *Christianity from Within* (Hodder & Stoughton, 1965).

work, sex, religion and the responsibilities of manhood in the tribe are compounded together in the training and initiation ceremonies for adolescents, so religious conversion sometimes plays a role in personality development, pulling its strands together and releasing energies towards a given goal. Because so much can be said in a negative way about adolescent religious conversion this must be said in a positive way. The techniques of ideological brain-washing and the parallels they offer with religious conversion in certain circumstances, the understanding and use by skilled operators of crowds, loneliness and fear, and the blunting of the critical faculties of the mind, all galvanize our determination to have nothing to do with any power that exerts pressure on personalities whose inviolability should be guarded at all costs. Conversion in the sense of a conversion experience in a mass situation is not a powerful force in the development of personal religion today, nor are revival meetings regarded as a means of church renewal, precisely because too much is known about the darker side. But conversion in the sense of the ability to make a new start and change the direction of one's life points to a human need that cannot be swept away with impunity.

What then are some of the organized means by which individuals both search for a personal belief and for the renewal of faith in its relation to the world? It is possible here only to distinguish a few types of activity and within these to state a few examples.

First, the use of large concourses of people for purposes of spiritual renewal, education and the discovery of new community. One could mention many official meetings that fulfil that purpose such as the Vatican Council and the Lambeth Conference and the Assemblies of the World Council of Churches. Even official delegates of churches need renewal. But these concourses are not open to all comers. Within the Roman Catholic Church there have been two Eucharistic conferences attended by the Pope, one at Bombay in 1964 the other at Bogotá in 1968. These concentrate on the renewal of worship and convey the sense of a vast worshipping community. The German (Protestant) 'Kirchentag' is held every year or two years and attracts hundreds of thousands; the highest attendance was half a million. It began in 1954 as the result of the vision and persistence of one man, a former professional soldier, an unwavering opponent of Nazism (and neo-Nazism) and a member of the secret 'confessing' church, Reinhold von Thadden. His aim was to prevent the German churches which had led a life of keeping quiet in Nazi times from continued self-preoccupation. With the division of Germany the church remained the only organization covering the two countries. Until the East German authorities clamped down strictly on participation, the Kirchentags were great reunions of separated relatives and friends and a demonstration of the unity of the church in spite of political divisions. One Kirchentag was held in East Germany. Each gathering, lasting more than a week, is prepared for by congregations and groups long in advance and organized round a particular subject. It proceeds by the method of few large meetings and services and very many small meetings and seminars including a number of international ones. The Kirchentag has succeeded in making many German people look out towards the world. The organization of the German churches for relief and development is one of the largest and owes much to the remaking of faith brought about by the Kirchentag in the lives of many people and some congregations.

Young people have always derived much from large concourses, often their first experience of exchange of views with others. Student conferences have affected the life of churches through their influence on their future leaders. But they have radically changed. In 1968 a Youth Conference sponsored by the British Council of Churches adjourned after two days 'to clarify its aims'. The conference programme was abandoned and in small groups the participants argued and prayed until at last by do-it-yourself methods they had arrived at consensus. Such an event puts a question mark against the usual conception of 'a well-organized conference' and indicates that the higher general level of education among young people than among many of the older religious professionals and adherents is not sufficiently taken into account.

Conference techniques for working out personal positions are not limited to religious bodies. One significant enterprise was the series of 'Present Question' conferences which began in the late forties and continued for six or seven years. With distinguished speakers and leaders they explored a number of moral, social and religious issues in an open way. Their reports, made into volumes of essays, gave wider circulation to the ideas expressed. No comparable meeting-place between humanists, religious believers and uncommitted persons now exists.

The 'march' is a new type of concourse: its aim is protest. Marchers (as the Aldermaston marchers experienced) become a kind of community. This one, although it originated in 'Christian Action', the movement started by Canon John Collins, contained people of many different backgrounds with a common concern for nuclear disarmament. Splits about aims and methods and especially about the use of violence destroyed the earlier unity and brought the marches to an end. From the public point of view the earlier demonstrations were the best in making their point. Perhaps the march cannot be institutionalized.

No march, it is safe to say, has had such far-ranging results as the 'march on Washington' of 250,000 people in support of the campaign for civil rights for negroes. The marchers were the congregations and ministers of negro churches and other supporters of the campaign: they were fed and lodged by negro congregations on their route. Seen by millions on television the march portrayed what it was asking recognition for, the dignity of the black man. The negro spiritual, the song of the oppressed, took on a new note: 'we shall overcome', confident but not brash. The march on Washington gave the decisive push to the movement which caused Congress to pass the Civil Rights Bill in 1968 – but not before the leader of the march, Martin Luther King, and John and Robert Kennedy had been murdered. In relation to civil rights the negro still has not regained the position he had in the period after the civil war called the 'Reconstruction' when there were twenty-two negro members of Congress and many in other offices in state and local government. After the recapture of southern government by pro-Confederate forces every negro lost office and none returned for fifty years. The church has been the only organization that was the negro's own, the minister the only negro not dependent on an employer for his livelihood. Many grew lethargic and some corrupt: subservience can be bought. The movement, beginning with the Montgomery bus boycott and culminating in the march on Washington under the leadership of Martin Luther King, gave many congregations a new life and they turned with energy not only to continuing the campaign for the registration of negroes as voters but to many direct action campaigns, to education (literacy, scholarships for able young people), legal defence and bail for negroes imprisoned for participation in civil rights programmes and campaigns against housing discrimination and job-discrimination. It is widely said that non-violent methods of protest have come to an end: that Martin Luther King was under pressure to use other means: not in the churches, nor, by a late opinion poll, by an overwhelming majority of negroes. The future will tell whether here in Britain as in the United States, we become the agents of bringing about what we fear ('the race war is bound to come') or triumph over our fears by the humble will to understand and an inflexible determination to build.

Second, there is the permanent institutional form of centres for renewal. I have already described the work of the evangelical academies in Germany: there are at least twenty other centres in Europe and in the United States, four in Canada, five in Great Britain, and centres in Africa, Asia and Latin America. Their characteristics are their lay emphasis and the combination of new searching into religious truth with preparation for new types of service. In developing countries they often work closely with governments in training personnel for such things as community development, adult education, agricultural advisory services, family advice services to help women coming from rural areas to mining and industrial areas, literacy programmes, preparation of literature for rural development and of programmes for radio (the churches own a radio station in Ethiopia able to broadcast to all central and eastern Africa and parts of the west). All such things as these are renewal of faith by discovering how faith is made active in the modern world. This is only a small part of all that might come under this heading.

Thirdly, there is withdrawal. This is characteristic of all religions: the forests and deserts are the symbols of it and may even be the places of it, occasionally, even now, as they were frequently in the past. One modern example of the birth of new faith and life from such withdrawal springs from the life of Charles de Foucauld. The life of this French cavalry officer who became a priest, then a monk and finally retired into the Sahara as a hermit seemed to issue in nothing that might ever affect the life of the church. He simply prayed, studied languages and offered his friendship to the Mohammedan tribesmen and the French soldiers who came his way.[1]

---

[1] CHARLES DE FOUCAULD, *Spiritual Biography* (New York, P. J. Kennedy & Sons, 1964).

When he was assassinated in 1916, perhaps by mistake in the course of a local war, it seemed that he would be soon forgotten. But years later the 'Little Brothers' and the 'Little Sisters' emerged. They follow the pattern of his life in that they spend a time of preparation in the desert and then they go to live in small groups alongside the poor. They work as the local people work and live by what they earn, they do not preach or teach or organize good works: they simply offer friendship. There are groups of them all over the world – among pygmies, in a fishing village in Alaska, on junks among the others on which refugees live on the river in Hong Kong. Their life of prayer, work and friendship is a corrective of the activism of the organization mind. From them has developed the idea of 'Christian presence': withdrawal in the midst of the world. The Protestant community at Taizé would be another example of the monastic life in the modern world. Their work for better understanding between Christians and their modern forms of worship, their open approach to secular knowledge and friendship to non-believers bring them many visitors seeking periods of withdrawal. In India the *Ashram*, Hindu or Christian, plays a similar role as the home of a small community and a place of prayer and withdrawal.

Lastly, the innumerable groups meeting in homes or for the occasional weekend in a residential centre simply cannot be described because of their number and variety. Their connection with local churches may be close, but is often distant. Books play an important role in bringing people into such groups. Many form around the books of a particular author and then dissolve. Many are mixed groups of believers and non-believers whose questions stimulate one another. 'Sensitivity training', a modification of group dynamics, is used by churches in North America, Great Britain and Australia to promote small group techniques in schools, congregations and neighbourhoods.

In a number of Eastern European countries, including especially Hungary, Czechoslovakia and the DDR there have been very active groups of Christians and Marxists: their topics of discussion are the humanization of socialism and the recovery of the human dimension in industrial societies.

The growth of the ecumenical movement has not only stimulated interdenominational and inter-faith groups: it has given pause to (though it has not stopped) what was a common feature in the history of protestantism, namely that any disagreeing group would break away and form a new church or sect with its own professionals and adherents. But there have for many centuries been protest movements against organization *as such* in religion, and these continue. One of the most interesting is the Japanese 'No Church'. It has no organization, professionals or sacraments. It is simply a number of groups each known by the name of its leader. They study the Bible and pray together; they write commentaries on the Bible (learning Greek or Hebrew to do so), but they do nothing that might lead them to organize. Some of the leading intellectuals in the country belong to the No Church. There are in other religions also those personally led groups, as for example some of the groups that promote Hindu Bhakti (devotion), which meet privately. All these contrast with the larger organized groups described earlier.

This chapter reaches no conclusion about the continuance and form of organized religion. The examples given lead to the conclusion that Christianity is in a peculiarly vulnerable position in today's world because unlike other great religions it is less diffuse, less a cultural style, more a societal belonging which became the cultural styles (in the plural) of Europe. A societal form is the butt of all the criticisms of 'religion': it has an address to which they can be sent. But it may turn out that the religions that are diffused through cultures will need everywhere *new* groups as the old culture patterns at least partly dissolve with economic and social change: there are many signs of this in Buddhism.

If we admit that to some considerable extent thought about God or about a transcendent dimension in life is influenced in its form and language by the structure of society, then times of social change are *necessarily* times of doubt and uncertainty about how to express such ideas, and of questioning as to their validity and usefulness to man. Doubt and questioning may be response to changes that at first sight have nothing to do with doctrines. What seems to me most hopeless is that adherents in a state of questioning should behave like Berdyaev's ineffectual liberal colleagues in the pre-revolutionary period who at three in the morning would cry 'but we can't do anything: we haven't settled the question of God yet'.[1] Abraham, though more mythical a character, is like many myths a surer guide: for by getting up and going he found what he did not know was there to look for, a feat that Plato (as he described in the *Meno*) believed impossible.

The peculiar organizational position of Christianity is that it exists in the form of societies of adherents inter-linked throughout the world, and newly aware of that connection. Many of these societal forms exist in cultures still impregnated by their faith. Societal adherence has a wide penumbra of cultural adherence: the word 'church' belongs to both. These societies have a kind of love–hate relationship with that culture, now rejoicing in it, now deploring it. Others of the societal forms of Christianity exist in cultures not influenced at all by their faith, or if so not in the same way: all of them are concerned with their surrounding culture because they share it with others as fellow citizens and are not satisfied with the rejection of it enjoined on them by their separate history as societies.

[1] NICOLAS BERDYAEV, *Dream and Reality*.

Supposing action were taken on given insight and the world-wide presence of these Christian societies called 'churches' were taken as a sign to act on behalf of man across the divisions of race and nation and class? Would that be accepting Mr. H. J. Blackham's advice to the churches that they might find themselves a new role as service agencies? I think not: because I believe it to be among the profounder theological insights of our day that God is to be found in the midst, not on the peripheries of life and that worship is renewed only by contact with its Object.

VII

JESUS

IT is not the aim of this chapter to outline or discuss the Christian doctrine of the person of Christ. There are many books that do this admirably. The context of this chapter is not Christian theology but on the one hand religion in its diverse manifestations and on the other the scientific study of religion as it relates to the documents of the New Testament and reacts on faith.

In a chapter of his book *The Gothic Image* Emile Mâle comments on the representations of Jesus Christ that appear in the sculpture, carving and stained glass in French cathedrals and churches of the thirteenth century. The century of St. Thomas Aquinas and of Chartres is rightly regarded as the pinnacle of the Middle Ages in the development of Christian philosophy and the achievement of religious art. Professor Mâle first comments on what is omitted from these representations when they are compared with the life of Christ as it is told in the gospels: he then turns to the way in which what is selected is treated.

The omissions are all the active ministry of Jesus, the teaching and healing, the travels with the disciples in Galilee and Judaea, the encounters with the Jewish authorities in synagogue and temple. The only occasional exceptions are his baptism, transfiguration and the marriage at Cana, and incidents in his life that appear as part of the lives of saints. Only four of the forty parables are illustrated. These constitute not a 'life of Christ' but illustrations of the days and seasons of the liturgical year. So tight is this tradition that even manuscripts of the gospels have many pages totally unadorned, though their matter could so easily invite the artist's imagination.

Equally remote from modern ways of thinking is the treatment of many of the incidents that do appear. The infant Jesus often lies not in a crib but on an altar and Mary's face is turned away or fixed on some distant point, as she contemplates the mystery that has been told her. At the side of the cross she stands crowned as the church, the chalice in her hand receiving the water and blood of baptism and the eucharist, while at the other side of the cross there sometimes stands the drooping female figure of the synagogue letting fall the broken tables of the law. The cross itself is at times the tree of the knowledge of good and evil, planted in Eden, and the blood of Christ flows over the skull of the old Adam. For centuries the symbolic and allegorical interpretations of the Bible had been growing. Every detail, regardless of propinquity of time or place, was woven into one intricate whole interpretation of the central themes of man's fall and redemption. The artist worked within this tradition, from which derived the marvellous artistic unity of the age. This is all a long long way from 'the quest of the historical Jesus' in the Biblical texts which has now for a century or more occupied the minds of scholars and many others. It is also a long way from the 'life of Jesus' which has been, and still is, a main ingredient in religious education in church and school.

There has never been *a* way of thinking or feeling about the person Jesus Christ. Modes of thinking have changed from one age and place to another with cultural background, even if the formal doctrines held among Christians about his person have remained more or less constant. Religious experience has varied too, not only from one age to another but from one person to another: this is now better understood, in the light of psychology, than it ever was before.

The Church of the Middle Ages regarded the understanding and interpretation of Jesus as her prerogative and hers alone: the expression of private judgement was not permissible and the possibility that Jews or Muslims might have thoughts about him could only be explored, if at all, on the peripheries of Christendom. Only very recently has it been recognized that in so far as Jesus is considered by Christians to have a message of universal significance all men must in some way have encountered the questions to which he is thought to be the answer, or had the life experiences to which he might be an illumination.

Understandings of Christ outside the Church

Christians are being compelled to recognize that men of other faiths and none make their own response to the knowledge they have of Jesus. The Church cannot force its understanding of him upon others. He is known, in varying senses of that word, far outside the Church, and honoured beyond its confines. 'In our present times' writes an Indian 'Christ has become a loved and worshipped figure for many in our country. Yet Hindus do not accept Christ as presented by the Church'. The Bible, translated into several hundreds of languages, is by far the most widely read book in the world, even in these secular days. It presents Christ, but not without interpretation. What is that interpretation and whose is it and what does it mean for today? New translations abound and all of them add something to understanding what the text says: but sometimes the very clarity of the language makes the meaning more, not less, mysterious to modern minds. It is not the case that a clear-thinking Church confronts a confused world; there are questions for believers too. There is always a possibility of new encounters with this figure of Christ: re-interpretations and new rejections. The walls of the Sorbonne in May 1968 bore evidences of both.

How often the Church has stood in its own light! The hold that the Church claimed, and to a large extent achieved, on all expressions of thought in the later Middle Ages meant that new ideas had to struggle not only against common human apathy and suspicion of new ways of thinking and living but against the Church. If the Church had not had such a hold on intellectual life (and indeed the whole of culture) would such a bitter struggle have been necessary? Why has the coming of science and technology to other countries and cultures outside the West precipitated no comparable conflict? Perhaps because these new forces did not grow up within those cultures and therefore could not appear as a threat in the same way. But that cannot be the whole reason; one is driven to the conclusion that an unusual degree of domination by religion over culture made it *inescapable* that a change in culture such as was brought about by scientific thinking and discovery was seen as a threat to the authority of religion.

Within the New Testament itself Christian faith is balanced on a knife-edge between its other-worldly and this-wordly elements. On the one hand is the Jesus who declares that his kingdom is not of this world; on the other the Jesus whose parables speak trenchantly of the obligation to serve one's neighbour, whose teaching and life alike speak of a love that goes beyond duty, and has its indestructible source in God. Christianity is rightly spoken of as 'world-affirming'. Yet once given power by the succession of events following the conversion of the Emperor Constantine how rarely and how feebly did the authoritative representatives of the Church resist the temptation to world-domination. The conviction that the Church *had* to be right justified in the eyes of many not only the defence of Europe against the Moors but the aggressive enterprises against Islam, against Eastern Christians and against heretics.

This is by no means just a matter of past history, nor just of Church history. Aggression is no doubt a factor in the make-up of all men, but European historical development seems to have given more than common opportunities for its organized expression. The price of this reverse side of the coin of European dynamism has usually been paid by non-Europeans. One often hears it suggested that religion is one of the greatest dividing forces among men and that if only all peoples were much more secularized there would be less friction and more understanding. This is doubtfully true: there are very few exports of Europe to the rest of the world that are not suspect to a greater or lesser extent – parliamentary democracy, trade and even aid, and western education, culture and morals. The conflicts that are spoken of as inter-religious often have a strong element of race in them – as between Hindus and Moslems for example – and a history of the racial dominance of one over the other at some time in the past. For the future, any religion that is inter-racial and cross-cultural has an important positive role to play in relaxing the inter-racial tensions that have mounted so alarmingly in the last twenty years. The Church is inter-racial and potentially cross-cultural, but only half realizes the importance of its situation and how it could be used. Its position derives from there being *one* Christ and *many* acceptances of him.

Christianity has been the religion of Europe and of white men. Some of the incontrovertible facts about Jesus are that he was not white and not a European. He was a Semite, of the same racial stock as Jews and Arabs. He did not belong to a princely caste or an imperial country: he was a poor man who worked with his hands and a citizen of a small, shamefully treated colony. However, it will not do the churches any good simply to rehearse these facts in the hope that emphasizing *now* an aspect of Jesus to which they have not given much attention will put matters right. The trouble goes far deeper than methods of presentation: it is a question of the fundamental attitude of Christians and especially of Church authorities to other faiths. When Pope Paul VI visited Bombay in 1964 he was greeted by huge and enthusiastic crowds, amongst them many non-Christians. His public speech with its quotations from the Upanishads was well received. But when he had gone the old doubts returned and one organ of Hindu opinion was asking whether he was not still the representative of a Church which fundamentally wanted to destroy Hinduism but had to admit that the old methods had failed. Not long afterwards an Indian bishop was commending the methods of the seventeenth-century Jesuit, de Nobile, who, after twenty years of fruitless preaching and teaching, took the dress of a Brahmin and spent his time with the Brahmins in the temples, listening as much as he talked. Before he died there were many Christian believers among them. Early in the present century a prominent English student of Hinduism wrote a book called *The Crown of Hinduism*, a study of the relationship of Christ to Hinduism along these lines. It was received with a good deal of hostility among some missionaries and leaders of churches in India because of the ever-present fear of syncretism, a subject much too vast to broach here and an ever-present reality in the religious situation of most countries of the East. However what was scarcely noticed at the time of Farquhar's book was the presence in India of a Christian church which had survived at least thirteen centuries of exposure to its surrounding Hindu neighbours in the southern state of Kerala. The Orthodox Syrian Church owed nothing to missionary expansion, Catholic or Protestant. The 'discovery' in recent years of this and several other ancient churches has helped to strengthen the growing conviction that the Christian communities which were planted by the emissaries of the Christian

West can and must become re-rooted in the cultures that surround them and related in a new way to the living faiths of other men.

This is already happening and promises to continue and increase. Study centres exist specifically for inter-religious study and understanding. In many ways science has assisted this development. The first contribution was the study of texts, using scientific methods of dating, comparing and deciphering: this was supplemented by work in the fields of archaeology and anthropology and all that makes up the modern study of religions as historical and living entities. The second is of a different kind – the objective reality of a challenging scientific view of the world to which intelligent exponents of religion have to relate. Thirdly and more recently the human sciences have shown that every individual is a microcosm as rich and diverse as the macrocosm of nature. Interest shifts from comparing *ideas* of which people are the mouthpieces to a personal encounter between *men* whose beliefs help to make them what they are. While scientific knowledge increases awareness of the complexities and varieties of human personality and helps to illuminate the way in which people accept and hold beliefs, yet each person, and he alone, can say 'I am myself: I alone know what it feels like to be myself'. The ordinary traffic of human en-counter from buying shirts to making love makes use of cultural conventions. Groups who share beliefs share a coinage for talking about them which both reveals and shields the individual. There is by definition no common cultural coinage for communication between cultures: meet-ing 'just as human beings' often breaks down for lack of recognition of this fact.

Those who are now trying to meet men of other faiths in a new relationship describe the situation as needing on their part a thorough study of the scriptures and the religious practices of others for these are formative influences on men and the vehicles of their religious experience. But in order to go further than this in communication they describe it as necessary to identify their own presuppositions and to 'put them into brackets for the time being' in order to concentrate completely on listening to the other without thinking how one is going to answer or argue with him. Christians who have had close touch with widely different areas of Hindu life and spirituality (urban and rural, sophisticated and simple) are able to say that it is in relation to Christ that they have been 'enriched in our contact with living Hinduism'.

Scientific Study of Religion and its Relation to Living Faiths

It is at present easier for the man of faith who wants to come nearer to a fellow human being by trying to communicate with him as another man of faith to acknowledge that he needs the knowledge that science gives, than it is for the scientific student of religions to admit that he has anything to gain from religious insight as such. This is partly due to the scholar's fear of being thought unscientific and partly to the way in which the scientific study of religions has developed. Writing about the XIth Congress of the International Association for the History of Religions, Professor Charles Adams[1] says that many nineteenth-century students of religion concentrated on primitive religions out of a conviction that here a 'purer' strand of religion could be found, something nearer to a primitive human religious drive. Even now the study of the phenomenology of religion concentrates on the archaic and, among present-day phenomena, on the primitive. 'There is implied', he writes, 'an order of priority and significance that would turn (and in fact has turned) scholarly

[1] CHARLES J. ADAMS, 'The history of religions and the study of Islam', in *The History of Religions*, edited by J. KITAGAWA (University of Chicago Press).

attention away from a large area of man's religious experience. In spite of their richness and immediate relevance to our own lives, the more developed traditions and particularly their contemporary evolution, seem to have been relegated to a background position ... delegates also expressed themselves as the congress proceeded as being suspicious of the genuine scholarly character of any study of religion in the recent past, not to speak of the living present. He asks very cogently what is the point of studying the archaic survivals of more primitive religion in Islam and ignoring 'the elements that went into the formation of the brilliant Islamic civilization of classical and medieval times'.

Professor Adams then made three points about the present-day study of Islamics. First, that modern communications have destroyed the closed world of the scholar: 'What is said in Chicago or written in Montreal is read in Cairo and Karachi. The response is immediate and strong and moreover it is important. ... the Islamicist now finds himself drawn into personal relationships with the modern representatives of the tradition he is endeavouring to study. ... If he is alive to human feeling he does not deal lightly with the most precious insights and values of others ... as a scholar he is also under obligation to be true to his own best insights. A Western Islamics scholar does not speak from the perspective of Islamic faith but whether he will or not he enters into communication with persons who receive his words and respond to them in the light of such faith'.

The second point derives from the first. Whatever the scholar puts forward will be searchingly examined by those who themselves profess Islamic faith. When the scholar says that a given institution, doctrine, practice or development is thus and so, and the Muslim replies that he cannot recognize these descriptions, what implications has this for the scholar's assessment of the value of his own study? He will not be shaken by the opinions of ignorant or narrow-minded men but he cannot brush aside 'the responses of learned and sober Muslims of good will'. It is true that sometimes the outsider enjoys an advantage in the attempt to win a critical grasp of a religious tradition and its development. But in relation to the immediate past and even in relation to the more remote, the Muslim is the inheritor of a tradition which still lives in him. The scholar therefore has to try to narrow the difference in understanding between the scholarly and the religious; to make the one insight reflect upon the other; not to admit to a duality of truth.

His third point can be more briefly put: the scholar of a religion whether he wants to or not becomes a participant in that religion's development. The work done on discovering forgotten customs and ceremonies, recovering and decipher-ing lost texts, has contributed to Muslim piety, enhanced Muslim self-understanding and increased confidence in the riches of the Islamic inheritance.

The point of making these quotations is that they say in terms of another religion what needs to be said about Chris-tianity. Scholars' work is becoming widely known: it poses the question of the truth of religion as seen to scholarship and as held by faith: it affects the development of religion. The points are easier to make about the relation of scientific study to a non-western faith because the western scholar is rarely a Hindu or a Muslim believer: but what about the situation where the scholar is also a believer? He is exposed to attacks from both sides: the secular scholar with no religious belief says with varying degrees of emphasis that the Christian scholar may be, is, or must be, biased in his scholarship to-wards a desire to defend the faith, while fellow-believers will be found in plenty to accuse him of undermining the faith of the faithful or even taking down the whole edifice of belief brick by brick.

The situation could be made a good deal easier if there were more scholars from other religions, trained in western methods, who would undertake such studies. Some are to be found, such as Radhakrishnan who combines the office of a profound philosopher of religion with that of a forthright advocate and modernizer of Hinduism. As a critic of Christianity he is worthy of the utmost consideration, and if Christians feel that he often gets the matter wrong, that only makes just the point made by Professor Adams above and illustrates for them what Hindus and others suffer from the more numerous and facile interpretations of Hinduism that Christians are prone to make. It is not possible as yet to match the particular kind of study of religion that has been done in the West by an equal contribution from the East: the precise and detailed study of texts is less attractive as yet to Orientals than the philosophical approach which is central to their own tradition.

The claim to universality that Christians make which, as Dean Inge said, 'is based upon and explained by the universality of Christ', constitutes the main reason why the reciprocal study of Christianity by non-Christian scholars should be taken much further. Many thoughtful people, including many Christians, regard it as a crippling disability in Christianity – a kind of amputation – that it has no place in its scheme of things for the insights of other religions. Simone Weil, who described her experience of Christ in language strongly suggestive of all Christian mysticism, stayed outside the Church all her life. 'In my view', she wrote,[1] 'Christianity is catholic by right but not in fact. So many things are outside it, so many things that I love and do not want to give up, so many things that God loves or they would not be in existence. All the immense stretches of past centuries . . . all the countries inhabited by coloured races: all secular life in the white

[1] SIMONE WEIL, *Waiting on God* (Routledge & Kegan Paul, 1951).

people's countries: in the history of those countries, all the traditions banned as heretical: all those things resulting from the Renaissance. . . . I should betray the truth, that is to say the aspect of truth as I see it, if I left the point where I have been since my birth, at the intersection of Christianity and everything that is not Christianity'.

Probably there are more people who share her point of view now than there were when this brilliant young French philosopher, who died in England in 1943, wrote those words. There are signs of change: there are institutions under religious as well as under academic auspices to promote study and exchange. The new Dutch Roman Catholic catechism which has created such a stir devotes several passages to other religions. The tone of its references is modest and conservative, but for such a thing to appear in official church teaching within one country which then gets widely read all over the world is something new. In Rome since Vatican II a secretariat for other faiths has been set up and books from Roman Catholic presses in which other faiths are seriously treated are by no means uncommon.

A new climate is needed and could be created, formidable though the difficulties are, in which men could meet as men conscious of their growing and developing humanity and of their role as the living agents rather than the passive repositories of religious beliefs which, viewed as 'systems', are irreconcilable. In religious dialogue the contribution of Christians is necessarily what is unique and central to them: Jesus Christ. It may be true as Professor R. C. Zaehner[1] says on his own considerable authority (referring to developments in Hinduism, Islam and Buddhism that are at variance with their scriptures), that 'there is in man a craving for an incarnate God strong enough to force its way into the most

[1] R. C. ZAEHNER, *Foolishness to the Greeks.* An inaugural lecture in the University of Oxford (Clarendon Press, 1953).

unpromising religious systems', what is certainly true is that thoughtful men everywhere are seeking for an understanding of the human dimension deep enough and strong enough to stand against those tides in the modern world that threaten man.

The Scholars' Study of the Records of Jesus

The central and unique affirmations of Christianity have to do with faith in a Jesus who lived in a particular country at a particular time. That faith grew up within a community which left no documents about him that are contemporary with him. Even the earliest are copies of copies. What were the originals? What in the documents we have reflects the faith and experience of a community, what is in any modern sense hard evidence about the object of their faith, Jesus? As Professor Leonard Hodgson puts it, 'What must the truth be, and have been, if it appeared like that to men who thought and wrote as they did?'[1]

The documents of Christian history have been studied from early times. But the eighteenth century marked the beginning of the modern approach. As soon as the Enlightenment gave birth to a scientific study of history *this* piece of history became an object of its inquiries like any other. The tools used and the subject matter of inquiry are, for example, the study of ancient tongues, the discoveries of archaeology, the painstaking techniques of analysing and comparing documents and relating them to possible places and dates of origin, the comparisons of ideas in philosophy and in religion in the Greco-Roman world, the various movements in Judaism before and after the time of Christ, the more ancient world in which the Old Testament was written and, behind that, the world in which the events that it describes took place:

[1] LEONARD HODGSON, *For Faith and Freedom*, pp. 87–8. Gifford Lectures (S.C.M., cheap edition, 1968).

these are some of the means and some of the subject matter
of the historical approach. The effect of acquiring it is like
watching the play *Rosencrantz and Guildenstern Are Dead*. The
minor characters take the stage: but the ancient world instead
of dying of boredom waiting to be caught back into the
mainstream of the plot appears full of life and interest, neither
aware of nor dependent upon the 'sacred history' going on
in its midst. The scientific historian's perspective inevitably
reduces for us the *scale* of that history which our forefathers
took to be *the* significant history, of which the person of
Jesus was the historical centre (standing between the past
Israel and the future Church) and the interpretative key.

Yet this change of scale is by no means all loss even from
the religious point of view. It points to the conclusion that
religious insight almost always arises in obscurity. It takes us
back again into something more like the world in which
Jesus was born, where Judaea and Galilee were insignificant
territories on the border of what was reckoned to be the
civilized world. As the ancient world comes before our eyes
as something real in itself, so also does other history and
culture. Was it not first an ignorant and then later a distorted
view of the Bible that taught it as *world* history? It is good to
be rid of such myopic views, and all sorts of other views are
beginning to follow it – all the separate histories of nations
and churches and parties and classes, with which they bol-
stered their morale and shielded themselves from seeing
themselves as others saw them. The hope that the professional
historian could give in relation to any of these histories 'the
unvarnished facts' proves very difficult to fulfil. Interpretation
is not only thicker than varnish, it is a different kind of thing.
Without understanding, facts are not so much like truth as
they are like a great dead slag-heap. The problem of getting
at the whole truth of a person's life is not one whit easier than
getting at the truth about a person in the flesh: all mere facts are

dead: all understandings have their presuppositions whether they are made by historians, psychologists or anyone else.

A hundred years ago Jesus was the enigma in a world of historians who had greater confidence in the finality of their judgements than many of them have today. It is difficult to imagine any modern historian, whatever his views about religion, writing the *Life of Christ* that David Strauss published in Germany in 1838 and which made such a stir in England when George Eliot's translation of it appeared in 1846. For he took the whole complex of varying types of material, sources and authorships that make up the gospels and reduced them to conformity with one principle: it was all myth. But even so he did not differentiate between the different meanings of that umbrella word. In modern parlance that 'Life' could have been called an 'anti-Life', for its conclusion was that a life of Jesus could not be written from the available sources.

Since that time 'the quest for the historical Jesus' as it is called, has gone on, not unremittingly (for activity has sometimes flagged), but with constant new injections of interest. Each point of view meets with correction by a successor, but the sheer weight of scholarship that has gone into many of these endeavours has left solid gains. Many books have been written summarizing the ebb and flow of the argument and assessing the work of the main participants in it. Albert Schweitzer, later known for his work as a doctor in West Africa and for his eminence as a scholar and exponent of J. S. Bach, published his *Quest of the Historical Jesus* in 1906 and thus gave a name also to a scholarly movement: but he did not inaugurate it. In his book, as in that of his more radical predecessor Johannes Weiss, the human Jesus comprehensible to a Thomas Arnold and millions of other 'Christian gentlemen' vanished to give place to a wild man of the desert preaching an other-worldly kingdom and an end of time in judgement and doom. But in England at any rate liberal views of a Jesus who could be written about by literary men, one not too hard to believe in, at least for the eyes of faith, and not too much of an affront to those looking for a moral guide, soon returned, only to be shaken again first by Karl Barth whose monumental *Church Dogmatics* had as its starting point God's total otherness and remoteness from man's natural being and thought,[1] and then by Rudolf Bultmann and others in the famous debate about de-mythologizing started by Bultmann's short manifesto *New Testament and Mythology*.[2] Bultmann's effort to remove from the gospel whatever belonged to the cosmological outlook of the first century in order that the essence of the faith might be more clear to the men of the twentieth resulted chiefly 'in giving the theologians some new meat on which to lay their eggs' (to quote a German bishop) so that the plain man was not edified nor were the theologians brought to a consensus. Soon a 'new quest of the historical Jesus' was under way, still in Germany, where the initiative has almost always been. A new look at the texts was combined with a sense of the responsibility of theologians in this field towards believers or potential believers. Was it tolerable, asked Bornkamm, that a man's faith should be made dependent on every twist and turn of scholarship? Though the ground for believing may not be in historical knowledge, nevertheless was it not possible to give an account of him that did not do violence to the strict canons of scholarship and yet made it clear that Jesus as a historical person had not totally vanished behind the smoke of controversy?

[1] KARL BARTH, *Church Dogmatics*, English translation (A. & C. Black).

[2] RUDOLF BULTMANN, 'New Testament and Mythology', the first essay in *Kerygma and Myth*, ed. HANS WERNER BARTSCH, English translation by Reginald Fuller (S.P.C.K., 1953).

But what emerges, and who benefits, and how much longer will the scholarly argument go on and find any interested readers outside theological circles? The discovery of the Dead Sea scrolls would surely not have excited such tremendous public interest had there not been the question of the light they might throw on Christian origins. Was the early Church prefigured by the Essenes and was Jesus even the 'Teacher of Righteousness' of this obscure, ascetic, political and apocalyptic sect of Judaism? With these discoveries assertions were at first made that there was in Jesus nothing original as to his teaching or even his death, but some of the more extreme of those statements have had to be withdrawn or dropped by their authors.

Jesus does not, as a result of all this, disappear into his environment. But equally it is now impossible any more to speak of his teaching and life outside that context. The 'Sabbath rest by Galilee' and 'calm of hills above' imagined in the popular hymn give place to Sir Maurice Powicke's description of Galilee as 'bordered by towns with temples and villas like the lakes of Geneva or Como today', and the context of the life shifts more to the wilderness of Judaea. The possibility of a connection between Jesus and the groups of men up against the powers that be, both Roman imperial and Jewish religious, grows more likely. The indications of a Palestinian origin of the tradition, oral or in small written collections of sayings, which later became the written gospels, grows surer.

The conclusion that there is not, and never will be, a way of seeing the historical Jesus except through the eyes of the early Church has in one sense never needed arguing. Nobody ever doubted that the authors of the gospels (i.e. those who collected and shaped oral and written tradition into the four gospels) were believing Christians: the question many posed was whether they were not over-believers, capable of persuading even themselves. Believers, however, in *what*? In the historical accuracy of the gospels as 'lives of Jesus' as nineteenth-century historians or churchmen would have understood 'history'? To ask the question is to carry back into the early Christian community categories that do not fit. That community had been brought to faith not by the recounting of the life story of a man Jesus and his claims. They believed that God had always been at work among men for their salvation. In Jesus they saw this happening in a way that fulfilled old hopes and broke old barriers. What had been for Jews was now for the whole world.

The gospels are not history that turns out at long last to be 'only religion': they were always religion, meant to speak of faith and to engender faith. They have a theological structure. To say that they are religious in meaning is not to say that they are historically worthless or untrue: they can be both historical and religious. Scholars will differ in their verdicts on particular passages. But those of which they can say 'this beyond all reasonable doubt describes what Jesus said or did' do carry a consistency. There is no biography, but there is the stamp of a real person on the memoirs. One begins even to understand why a generation of people who had never seen him felt for him love as well as the awe of faith.

Scholars and Believers

What happens if one tries to apply to Christianity what was said by Professor Adams about the inter-action between scholarly study of Islam and believing Muslims? He claimed as a scholar that the response of believers was important to scholars because the believers stand in a living tradition and are part of it. Can the same man both study his religion and respond to it as a believer, or does this lead to inescapable double-think?

Since Martin Buber wrote his little book *I and Thou*[1] there has been a shorthand way of talking about the difference between our relationship to what we study and master as an object ('I-It') and what we know in another relation, not that of subject to object but of subject to subject ('I-Thou'). Buber was not talking about the difference between our relation to things and our relation to people, nor of there being an outward physical life of people that we can know as we know an object and an inner life of the person that can only be understood by a sort of empathy. C. A. van Peursen[2] in his *Body, Soul, Spirit* points out that what a man likes to think of as his inner life is all too often objectively revealed to others by the slips and habits of which he is unconscious and he continues 'Man is no imprisoned mind, concealed from the world by a palisade (the body). His situation as an "I" is not one of isolation. On the contrary the other person is just what he cannot do without. Self-knowledge begins when he has contact with his fellows, and not before. *Because* the "I" is inalienable, because it cannot swop places capriciously with the other, it has need for him in his otherness'.

Men do know Jesus in both relationships. In so far as he is a problem to believers, the relation is 'I-It': in so far as he is a person even to one who would not call himself or be called a believer, the relation is 'I-Thou'. Both relationships have their place. But faith arises only from the second, as openness to this person subject-to-subject becomes the transforming *self*-knowledge of a relationship which includes and goes beyond the personal into faith and trust in God. To know all the facts in the gospels to be historically accurate accounts of real events would not necessarily engender faith. Liberated first from sentimentality and unreality by the historical

[1] MARTIN BUBER, *I and Thou* (T. & T. Clarke, 1939).
[2] C. A. VAN PEURSEN, *Body, Soul, Spirit – a Study of the body–mind problem* (Oxford University Press, 1967)

researches and debates of a century and now from dependence on the continual ebb and flow of those debates, faith stands on its own ground. But it is not blind faith: what attaches the Jesus-event to our own and any future day is its searching understanding of the human heart and a word spoken into the contemporary situation. For any of the persons mentioned in the gospels, 'contemporary' meant first-century Palestine: for us and our children it means today or tomorrow. If the words of Jesus and the life portrayed, so consistent with those words, do not 'speak', what does it matter whether he said them? Thus faith in Jesus always has this contemporaneity about it: a living Christ, not a 'historical Jesus', known in prayer and sacraments but also and increasingly in the revolutionary struggles of our time.

All over the world, wherever there is the fact or the memory of the domination of white races there appears the rejection of the white Christ and of the white man's church. The violence of this rejection has caused innumerable breakaways from churches of white leadership and the founding all over Africa and Latin America of indigenous churches, groups and movements. Some of these bring pre-Christian customs long suppressed into their worship, beliefs and moral conduct. All of them have taken from Christianity the motif of *Messianism*. It expresses exactly their own combination of longing and waiting, and certainty that their hour is close at hand. Messianism is to be found even where organized Christianity has had only marginal influence. From the cargo cults of many Melanesian islands to the Peyote cult of North American Indians, from the messianic movements of Brazil to the Bantu prophets of South Africa – they are all religions of oppressed people. 'The cry for freedom rising from the throats of the oppressed peoples is fraught with lessons for us to learn, for it inherently denounces the contradictions within our own culture as they appear to the new worlds now beginning to take shape.' So writes Lanternari[1] in his *Religions of the Oppressed*.

The contradiction within our western culture of which Lanternari speaks is between the white nations' wealth and dominance, expressing itself first in the enslavement of coloured peoples, then in colonialism and now in an economic pressure upon certain poorer nations which development aid scarcely mitigates, and the heart of the white nations' traditional religion which is Jesus. No one has articulated this contradiction more clearly than Martin Luther King who constantly pointed to the poverty and degradation of the black descendants of the white man's slaves as the sickness of a white society, richer and more powerful than any empire had ever been, which yet would not allow black people their basic rights as human beings. 'I think my people understood that figure hanging on his cross between two thieves better than your people' said the American negro writer James Baldwin.

If individual Christians and the organized churches are to respond to the clamant human needs of the time and join the struggle for peace and justice, for the poor and the under-privileged, then the Jesus they will see will be the coloured man, the defender of the poor, the judge of prejudice, who proclaimed and lived by a law of love. But nothing creative is ever born from guilt – only from a contrite disposition of the will which is then able to accept that one is loved and free to love. That is what faith in Jesus means.

[1] VITTORIO LANTERNARI, *The Religions of the Oppressed* (Mentor Books, 1963).

VIII

GOD

To ask whether God has a future is nonsensical. God, if he were a creature, object or ingredient in the time process could have his expectation of life or likelihood of survival calculated: in other words he would not be God.

Any making of God into an object renders him part of time and decay: that is it makes him not God. That God or gods are immortal both in the sense of not being human and not subject to death is world-wide belief about gods. Myths of dying gods contain their rising or return: gods that do not return are at most heroes.

It is arguable that all talk about God brings him into the realm of objects, and this is not a new problem either. An old Muslim proverb runs 'If you say that God is thus and so, I tell you flat, he is not that'.

To ask whether fifty or a hundred years hence men will *believe* in God is an entirely different question. One has often read statements to the effect that God would cease to exist when there was no one left to believe in him. What, after all, has happened to the Greek gods? People ceased to believe in them or worship them and turned to other gods. They do not exist as gods for us and we say 'they do not exist'. Did they die? Or if we say they never were true gods, they were false gods, no gods or idols or explanations of natural phenomena under the guise of myths, what are we saying about those who believed in them? That they were wholly deluded? That sounds arrogant. On the other hand to say that what the Greeks worshipped under the guise of the gods was the same reality as the Jews worshipped as Jehovah is to be false to the experience of both Greek and Jew. The difficulty cannot be got around by bringing in the word 'reality' in this connection, obliterating the distinction between A and B by saying that anyway there is only one real thing, C, and they are both like that. This use of the word 'reality' usually ends up by saying 'What is God? Reality. What is Reality? God'.

Nothing can defend us from the fact that all talk of God is talk by human persons. The mystic's first-hand experience of the divine, granting it to be that, becomes a human communication immediately anything is said about it. The question is whether talk about God is talk or mere talk. That question must be taken up later. The point is that, for example, we do not have to 'believe in' the Greek gods in order to think that the Greeks were talking about something vastly important in their experience. And all great religious ideas have something in them that speaks not only of experience in the conditions of a given time and place but of something more universal, shared by many or most men. When Freud uncovered the feeling of little boys for their mothers and how this could become in some cases obsessive, he called it the Oedipus complex – not just because this was the story of a man who by accident killed his father and married his mother, not knowing who she was, but because like Oedipus the boy is driven by powerful forces that he cannot understand or control. The Greeks externalized these as gods or furies while Freud internalized them. Thomas Hardy's novels often have an underlying tone of Greek tragedy: the characters are not free persons and their lives are, as Hardy himself said about Tess, the sport of the gods. Many people know just what Hardy was talking about, feeling as they do that life has dealt them blow after blow as though from some unseen hand indifferent to their feelings or their endeavours. In what sense therefore are the Greek gods dead?

But to return to the statement that God would cease to exist simply because there would be, perhaps in the foreseeable future, nobody left to believe in him.

There is one sense in which such a statement is true. Henri de Lubac remarked years ago that many people, whatever their professed beliefs, were 'practical atheists'.[1] Believing in God was so marginal to their thinking and behaviour that *for them* the existence or non-existence of God made no difference: they behave as though he did not exist; he might as well not. But it is still nonsense to assume that the practical or even the believing atheism of many, most or even all people could either cause or prove God to be nonexistent. God could exist if there were no believers: he could exist if there were nothing. But such statements cannot themselves be proved or disproved.

If disbelief does not prove the non-existence of God, neither on the other hand does belief prove his existence. The 'ages of faith' cannot be summoned as witnesses for the defence of God's existence: even universal belief in God could not make him exist or prove him to exist. The attempt to rest back on such arguments evacuates the term 'God' of what made it powerful to those who did believe, namely that they did not think that their belief was the source of God's being. What we consciously create we cannot believe to have an existence in its own right: even our children we speak of 'giving birth to', i.e. they are not our creation. But what we discover because we believe that something of the sort is there before we find it is a different matter.

Surveys of religious opinion and behaviour are not altogether reliable evidence on matters of such complexity as belief in God. They do, however, indicate that a great many people think that religion is a valuable source of social

[1] HENRI DE LUBAC, 'The New Man: the Marxist and the Christian View', *The Dublin Review*, first quarter, 1948.

cohesion and moral teaching. What they *really* want to see preserved is not so much God as all the things they think depend from some acknowledgement of his existence. They therefore support religious institutions financially and perhaps by official membership and occasional attendance and they want religious education to continue in schools. They often act as a conservative force in religion. They do not want changes in its forms and language; they dislike theological debate and religious controversy, they expect ecclesiastical authority to be conservative and firm; they do not want public doubt thrown on things about which they have private reservations.

Such people are not to be despised. They form an important counter-balance to those who think that belief in God is absurd and could vanish without any consequences of importance to society or the human person and should therefore be hurried out by every means available: who have no inkling of the despair and horror felt by Nietzsche as he faced the possibility of a 'death of God', nor any sympathy for that type of humanist who reads the sacred books of religion with understanding and knows how formidable are the problems of making good the loss of faith.

It is difficult to believe that anything of new creative religious thought could come from either of these extremes. Those who want to keep an acknowledgement of the existence of God officially in being for reasons of morality or order or cultural continuity are taking very short views. If their own diagnosis is correct and the things they care about really do depend on God as they say, then those things cannot be kept alive by belief in a dead God. A failure of the heart is bound to produce a collapse of the limbs. But perhaps some of them are really afraid that a living God would bring about changes in morality and give the cultural tradition an unwelcome twist into the future? Either way, their position has no future because a younger generation is not prepared to take it over: for the young 'a live dog is better than a dead lion'. Those at the other extreme who write off religion in general and God in particular as dead and useless often seem unable to leave well alone and while they ridicule and condemn they are scarcely ever prepared to check their facts about religion and so become the purveyors of half-truths and falsehoods.

Leaving on one side the factor of the enduring power of great institutions, the future in the sense of creative development seems to me to lie with a great variety of groups and individuals, within and outside the structures of institutional religion, namely with those who have a religious faith which is open to the world and ready for what comes; who are not prepared to let the idea of God go without wrestling with the profundity of it. The attitude of these persons I can only describe as a continuous willingness and endeavour to open up the textures of their own lives, and of the groups and institutions to which they belong so that neither thought nor ways of living become clogged and lumpish. An attitude of hope and a conviction that the material for new and creative enterprises arises out of common experience can hold in communication with one another people whose starting points are remote.

God and the Problem of Language

Difficulties about believing in God and about what the word itself might mean are by no means all intellectual. People can and do say that nothing in their experience has seemed to require or indicate what they understand others to mean by 'God': and there are others who say that they believe and do not need to argue. One takes them at their word: it is their experience. But there *are* problems that are intellectual, and these are properly a matter for discussion. What we call 'God', while it is not in origin a mental concept like a mathematical formula and does not function in most believers' lives primarily as such, has nevertheless had a great deal of intellectual content put into it by some of the greatest minds of the past: it has been greatly reasoned about qualitatively as well as quantitatively. The notion that the idea of God is being swept away by a recent flood of reason breaking against bulwarks of superstition is far from true. Superstition or 'blind faith' is peculiarly resistant to rational argument and it may very well be that the concept 'God' is vulnerable to intellectual argument precisely because it has had so large an intellectual content and has been so closely reasoned and invites reasoned assault.

Much has been written about problems of faith in God in relation to the development of science. I shall not go over this ground. But the question of the use of language, while it has certainly not gone undiscussed, is so fundamental to any discussion of what we mean by 'God' and 'belief in God' that I shall try to say some things about it both at the intellectual level and at that of common experience, the two being of course interrelated by being the activities of persons.

Philosophers first turned their interest to analysing the use of language not in order to attack theology or ethics but in the main for its bearing on their own work as philosophers and because of the importance of language, including the language of mathematics, in the development of science. In the last thirty years linguistic philosophers have asked 'what sort of talk is this?' about almost everything human beings might want to talk about. It could be shown by using these philosophical tools that many statements that were thought to be statements of fact were really value judgements, opinions, wishes, exhortations, exclamations or commands disguised by the structure of the sentence to look like plain statements of fact.

Talk about God has been so prolific, and its authors have so frequently and some of them so blandly assumed that whether accepted or rejected for truth the talk was meaningful, that the blows fell on a large target. The circularity, ambiguity and illogicality of many arguments were laid bare. Language about God and about values in both ethics and aesthetics had to stand comparison with the mounting successes of science in using language with precision for definition and communication and above all in making statements that are verifiable. Verification became the key issue and A. J. Ayer's *Language Truth and Logic*, published in 1936, stands as perhaps the chief example of the extreme position to which logical positivism could be pushed. It seemed to erect a sort of iron fence round what could be meaningfully discussed. All science fell inside it: most of ethics and aesthetics and all metaphysics, which meant nearly all the ways in which God was talked about, fell outside.

Many things have happened since the publication of that extreme but salutary book, including some modification of his position by its author. Philosophers' word games, although they were associated with Oxford where their rules were developed, have found players all over the West and uses in a number of disciplines: they apply vigour to the use of language and explore meanings. But for philosophy itself it is a limited life that waits for others to open their mouths in order to snap out 'Prove it', 'Illogical', 'No meaning'. The tendency of thirty or even ten years ago to stress the radical nature of the break with the past has given way to a reawakened interest in older philosophical ideas and the relevance of some of these to modern problems. More important, in spite of the prohibitions English philosophers have regained both the desire and the ability to talk about matters that fell outside the ring fence, especially about ethics. Their work seems guarded and useful rather than creative and dynamic.

Thanks to them (though it was David Hume who first made the point) it has become a commonplace now to say that no number of 'is-es' add up to an 'ought'; that values cannot be derived from facts or sense perceptions. Much emphasis is therefore laid on the making of personal value judgements and how this can be done without either unquestioning submission to authority (to submit knowingly to authority is of course a value judgement about that authority) or pure subjectivism (merely 'I prefer'). Yet one senses an unsatisfactoriness in a divorce between decision-making and things-as-they-are-in-themselves. Platonic idealism is 'out': no one it seems believes in the reality 'out there' of 'ideas' or independent entities of justice or beauty. But is there really nothing in the thought of a coinherence, a consistency of all the many acts of justice – no universality about it? Why do men who are fighting for justice in different parts of the world assume that this is a real goal and that others will understand them and join in?

From examining language in the sense of words and sentences in speech and writing and what they do and mean some philosophers have become intensely interested in language itself as a human faculty: this is also of interest to the professional students of linguistics. How comes it that, unlike computers, we utter from early childhood on meaningful sentences we never heard? How do we know that some things just do not 'go' in language, and find this out so early in life? Noam Chomsky in order to explain this says 'go back to another long discarded idea: the idea that there are faculties of the mind'. Here again something universal appears 'faculties *of the mind*', i.e. a mind common to all men, and in the mind a source of language competence, as it is called. This is quite different from some current ideas of language as the product of particular stimuli from a particular environment: language appears as creative achievement. The Hebrews said that. Not for them any images or visual arts, but they carried forward all their creative ideas in language until, quite late in their history, they were able to say that the world was made by a word spoken. In this they are not conveying insight upon the origin of the physical universe but on the given and shared nature of man, who does not just speak but *speaks out meanings*. Created by a word, man creates by speech. Some of this new talk about the mind sounds not unlike ideas St. Augustine expressed in his dialogue with his son (*de magistro*). St. Augustine says that as the eye cannot see itself but sees what it looks upon, so the mind illuminates what it reaches out to and cannot fathom what it is in itself or what its light is.

Chastened by rightful rebukes of meaningless talk can we talk about God? What do we really want to talk about? The word or a meaning? Suppose we become acquainted with two girls. One is called Grace, but unfortunately we do not catch the name of the other. Each meeting with the two of them makes it more certain that the one whom we are eager to know better is not Grace, who has the meaningful and self-giving name but the other one, who is in being gracious and friendly. What, we will ask, is in a name? It is the reality we are looking for: so we swallow our pride and address the gracious one. It could be like this in the matter of God: that the visual images of childhood, the pictures we drew and hymns we sang have the name attached to them, but that if we looked around our experience we would find that in it which we deem more worthy of a commitment than the child's old man in the sky or the angry authoritarian, or the indifferent world mechanic.

There are those who say 'our image of God must go': the old man in the sky must be burnt like Guy Fawkes and we must set out to find a new way of thinking of God. I do not see it quite that way. I have had experience of waiting on the platform for a train: it comes in, but from the opposite direction: I get in and it moves off. Nothing corrects the overmastering impression that I am headed away from my destination. Thinking back to the place I was in and the journey to the station only confirms my worst forebodings of lost connections and broken engagements. I try to read, I look out of the window. Suddenly without being able to say why or how I feel I am travelling the opposite way: the train, the rails, the scenery have all done a volte-face. I can in my mind now repeat my journey to the station mirror-wise. I believe this happens in relation to the experience of God. What one thinks one ought to believe contradicts or does not connect with a lot of what one experiences and most values in life: you do what is the practical right next thing (get on the train in spite of the nagging 'ought I not to have faith and go the other way?') and lived experience asserts itself as reality and reorganizes past experience into continuity with it.

This may well be a form of conversion experience in the modern world: that from searching the heavens to find God and attempting to be very spiritually-minded one slowly or suddenly becomes aware that what one needed but could not express was discernible by clues or flashes of insight or unexpected awarenesses as one's life was opened up to receive whatever would come largely unsought through events, sights, sounds, encounters, delights and afflictions. C. S. Lewis in the last pages of *Surprised by Joy* describes in unemotional language a ride on the top of a bus on the outskirts of Oxford. Something happened which he could only describe as the cracking of a tortoise-like shell which had always protected him from self-disclosure. He knew, against all the power of will mustered to prevent it, that the crack could not close. A friend recently sent me a poem he had written: a line of it reads 'God is the wound in my side through which I feel my neighbour'.

If language is a creative faculty, then we have to use it boldly to describe for ourselves and others whatever has the ring of truth and genuineness for us. By disciplining this use, bringing to bear on it a necessary economy and sincerity, we examine our lives, finding what frustrates and what enhances our knowledge and practice of truth and love. If we are open to the possibilities of language we will be sensitive to the use of it by others and recognize that others may be speaking of profoundly religious matters without using traditional language.

Nearly all religious teaching, however, is based on the input–output theory of language. From very early years children learn from religious parents or in school or church to use a religious vocabulary which scarcely ever latches on to their own experience. Many teachers and some parents are concerned about this and therefore begin to leave children more freedom to express in their own words and actions the feelings of awe and wonder, pity, sorrow, affection and gratitude that come to them. When they are taken to church they find themselves among adults who are using language to which many of them have become largely deaf: it is not their own. It may be the background of their own thoughts and the means of sharing in corporate acts. But one hears with increasing frequency not only of young adults but of middle-aged churchgoers who would describe what they feel about religious language in something like the words used to me by an Australian, 'Quite unexpectedly it seemed as though all that was uttered in church came showering down upon me in a cascade of empty sounds: I could not pick up and piece together anything *real* from it all. When I found others who in their own way were having the same experience, I asked myself what on earth could be done. I have not lost faith in God, but I can't *say* anything'. Many others would however say that losing the capacity to say anything about

God and losing faith in his existence were simultaneous experiences, or two parts of one experience. Others would say that the impossibility of talking the sort of language that talking of God seems to involve makes the faith they want impossible to come by.

How did man's expression of a relation to God come to be loaded with so many words? Surely the answer to this question would be a long history. Even today one can go to places where man's chief form of devotion is the performance of an action, individual or corporate: a garland of flowers at the shrine, the lighting of a lamp, pouring water, anointing with oil, laying on hands, the dance, the procession. What we have in the West is the result of a reforming and purging process in Christianity to get rid of or prevent superstition, to refine and articulate ideas as well as feelings, to bring religious worship into line with the increasingly word-using culture of Europe.

It is not necessary to *say* anything in the worship of God. Wordless prayer, or waiting on God are forms of worship. Sacraments involve the worshipper more deeply than many more highly verbalized forms of worship – but they become a mere indulgence in vague feelings of numinosity unless the worshipper understands and shares their meaning as memorials of and issues from events: and that involves the use of words. The Jewish passover meal with its recital of the escape from Egypt and the re-enactment of the events of the last night of captivity are a clear example of the historical element in an action whose religious meaning as worship is to bind God and people together in the present assurance of his presence.

These last two paragraphs illustrate the fact that religion is not a philosophy. The words of religious acts simply cannot be separated from the actions performed – even the movements of the body. The forging of a vocabulary and the wealth of symbolism come from reflection on their experience made by a continuing community of people. This has gone into the making of scriptures and responsiveness to *present* experience is a condition of understanding them. 'God' is a word with histories: the future has to contain an engagement with that past.

Nevertheless religious language used in or out of the context of worship has to be validated in experience, to be true to life. The trouble is that it does not, in part at least, validate itself in this way, and for two reasons. The first is that it contains very often a heavy ingredient of metaphysical language and this brings one up against the philosophical problems again. The second is that many people would never dream of putting into the sort of religious language they know things that happen to them in life which are meaningful and demanding of a response. But they have no alternative that measures up to what they need. Take the hymn often sung in churches and schools and used by some non-Christians also –

> Immortal, invisible, God only wise,
> In light inaccessible hid from our eyes,
> Most blessed, most glorious, the ancient of days,
> Almighty, victorious, thy great name we praise.

The only word that connects this with the everyday realities of life is the 'we' of the last line. Even the 'light' of the second line is not light as we know it. It is metaphysical language. But now take by contrast this folk song[1] –

> When I needed a neighbour, were you there, were you there?
> When I needed a neighbour, were you there?
> And the name and the colour and the creed don't matter,
> > Were you there?

[1] Words and music by Sydney Carter.

This is often sung by young people engaged in community service, on work camps and so on. It is non-metaphysical language. It expresses a common desire to help a neighbour in need and a challenge to others to join in. It does not compel anyone to go beyond these human relationships. Yet anyone who wants to do so can see even in these short lines references to the gospels. The 'I' is also Jesus who is served by every act of neighbourliness to anyone in need, even by those who do not know him, for the reference is to the parable of the last judgement – a highly metaphysical concept. The other reference is to the widening of the meaning of 'neighbour' from 'kith and kin' to 'all men regardless', taught by Jesus in the parable of the Good Samaritan. I repeat, the connection is not compelled. Then what is added by reading these religious overtones into it? A reminder of, or an incentive to look at, the New Testament exposition of the cost and meaning of love.

Public worship makes large use of metaphysical language. It needs to be interpenetrated with the language of practical experience giving voice to everyday contemporary feelings and concerns. This mixture corresponds very closely to the sacerdotal and the lay components of a body of worshippers. Private prayer can make far greater use of everyday speech. Prayer is not a matter only for convinced believers: it is also a way of finding out the meaning of experience by making it into words, seeing how far everyday language will go.

I once told a non-Christian friend that I had come across a number of young people who thought it was hypocritical to pray if you were not sure whether you believed in God. 'What nonsense' he replied 'how else would you find out?' If they shared the very common assumption that prayer is making petitions, then they were right. But if, on another view, the only possible language about God is language addressed to God, then he was. Once anyone begins to tell anyone else what prayer ought to feel like, he is back again pinning God down to particular descriptive language and substituting for an exploration of meaning a three-letter word. A slender thread of something of our own is the only thing that can connect any one of us to the riches of a religion. With the collapse of a cultural network there will need to be many such threads in the future.

IX

THE FUTURE OF MAN

ONE does not have to be of a deeply reflective disposition, given to pondering man's nature and destiny, but only a reader or viewer of the news that pours through the channels of the mass media, at least in the West, in order to ask oneself sometimes what is to become of man in the future.

Awareness of the fact of death, one's own certain destiny, characterizes every human consciousness. Since one can only die one's own death, the thought of mass annihilation in a nuclear or a race war is in one sense no more horrifying than the thought of one's own death. To die and make place for succeeding generations is a lot man shares with the animals and accepts consciously as the law of his nature. To die leaving no succeeding generations, to imagine oneself caught in the last holocaust is something of a different order. The precautions a man takes to preserve his own life, the hope and effort he puts into preparing his children to take their place in the world, count for nothing in the face of such a possibility.

On 6 August 1945 an American plane dropped on Hiroshima the first atomic bomb. The full horror of the human suffering caused only became known months later. On the day itself the announcement brought, even to people used to six years of nothing but war news, a sense of shock. Few people knew anything about atomic physics and military research was secret. The public was totally unprepared for what it heard. Something new, strange and terrifying in its possibilities had come into the world. It was soon recognized that the discovery of nuclear fission had no parallel in human history since the discovery of fire. Sir Lawrence Bragg, for example, one of Britain's leading physicists, spoke of the discovery of fire 'by which man found a way of bringing back at will the sun's warmth and light, stored up as energy in the fuel he burnt. But the latest atomic fire', he continued '. . . comes from a far more distant and awe-inspiring source than the sun's heat. It was imprisoned in the nucleus in some great cauldron when the stars were made, in regions packed with energy to an unimaginable extent. These prodigious forces wound up the springs which the atomic explosion releases'.[1] In radio talks and newspaper articles such as these people heard for the first time what is now common knowledge to every child doing general science at school. And at the same time those with an eye to the political future pondered the fact that the decision to drop the bomb had been taken by President Truman on his sole responsibility.

Since Hiroshima the nations have had to live with the power that was then let loose for the first time. Sir Winston Churchill expressed his view that, since the outbreak of nuclear warfare between the major powers would be a war in which there could be no victors, a balance of terror might prove to be the most powerful deterrent. In the last twenty years new weapons for the annihilation of man have been piled into the balance on both sides. The whole concept of 'a balance' also changes as new powers begin to make their own nuclear armaments and to take up the stance of defensive threat.

This is not the place to chronicle the slow steps made by governments and intergovernmental organizations to bring the situation under some sort of control by rounding certain critical corners without major disaster and by preventing the level at which the balance was kept from rising as fast as

[1] *The Listener*, 30 August 1945.

unrestrained competition would have allowed. Event after event however shows how real the threat continues to be: for small nations the price exacted or threatened in terms of loss of freedom or life itself is overwhelming. But it is to the purpose of this concluding chapter to mention those who have corporately acted to improve the chances of man's survival. First among these are the scientists who emerged as a voice in public affairs over the dropping of the first atomic bomb. The argument that it was their business to conduct research but that it was the moral responsibility of society to decide what use was made of it, could not stand in a situation where public opinion was unaware of the facts or of their possible consequences. Professor Einstein's letter to President Truman has become a classical document, but it has had many successors in actions by which scientists have urged on governments or on public opinion the consideration of the use of their work. No other group could have been so effective as they in such matters as pointing to the genetical effects of nuclear fall-out and thus bringing about a cessation of above-ground testing. As more and more of the fundamental research done in science is paid for by governments and especially (directly or indirectly) by their war departments, public opinion has been an important court of appeal for scientists. Not only the public interest but their own freedom is frequently involved in such issues. Other scientists have directed attention to different potential threats to man's health and safety: to the effects, for example, of heavy reliance on antibiotics in factory farming, and of toxic sprays in agriculture. Recently Sir Bernard Lovell questioned whether those who authorized or conducted space probes took enough account of the inadequacy of present knowledge about the possible effects on the earth of continuously puncturing the encapsulating and insulating skin of the atmosphere that surrounds it like a protective covering. No one but the scientists can raise with adequate knowledge such questions about man's future.

Writers and journalists have also come into a new position since the threat to men's survival and freedom became so apparent. Creative writers and intellectuals have always lived in communication with one another across national boundaries: they created an international literary community. But important as it was, it was always an élitist function. What is new now is the function of the writer and journalist in speaking to a vast popular audience. Professional standards of accurate reporting and fair comment are a moral force in the world. It is obvious that Soviet education has produced the possibility for there to be many more writers and a great reading public: both are suppressed.

The churches too use the fact of their existence as an international community to speak and work for peace in a variety of ways. Latest on the scene comes organized youth, organized to protest: some prepared to take violent action against authority and to try to change the actions of governments and some organized to serve internationally and to make a protest of a different kind.

These are only some of the examples that could be quoted of ways in which developing networks of communication are helping to make possible the growth of an international community. This is an essential but only a preliminary task. There is no security for mankind until force as the arbiter in international relations is brought under the control of law. Many years ago Mr. Lionel Curtis, a lifelong student of international affairs wrote the following:

> The reason why international law is not true law is not, as is often said, because it has no 'sanction' – because the Permanent Court of International Justice has no sheriff or police force to execute its decisions. That is an altogether secondary consideration. The real reason why international law is not true law is because

there is no community for it to function in. A community is a body of people held together by a common consciousness, a sense of togetherness.[1]

One of the conditions of participation in this effort to create such a community is the abandonment, not of convictions, but of ideology, that is of the claim that only on one's own basis can an international community be created. Both Christians and Marxists have made such claims, the one on the grounds of knowing *a priori* the conditions of human community and of having been, as Christendom, an international community of the past, and the other on the ground of the necessity of world revolution as the condition of creating world community. It was difficult for the Roman Catholic Church not to be drawn into an alliance with all anti-communist forces, whatever their political colour, on the ground of opposition to 'Godless communism'. The change that has come over Roman Catholic official utterances and actions in the last twenty years owes something to individual statesmanship, more to the presence within communist countries of large Roman Catholic churches which have to survive the accusations of being potential agents of counter-revolution, and most to the turning away from negative accusations to positive concern with peace and with justice for the human person whoever and wherever he is. As intractable ideological stances have been abandoned by Roman Catholics and other Christians, so one can speak of their *increasing* role in the creation of an international community.

Chairman Mao reviles Soviet leaders for their revisionism and their betrayal of Marxist principles. But it is all too clear from their actions that they do not feel safe in a world where there are powers which have not undergone communist

[1] 'The real and the ideal in international affairs', published in the *Christian News-Letter*, no. 235, 30 May, 1945.

revolution nor with allies who, having had their revolution, now seek under communist leadership to advance beyond it to a richer development for the lives of ordinary people. The discontent of younger Marxists with the pressure of the system upon the individual has led to the search for a 'humanization' of Marxism which would have the effect of reducing it from ideology to a way of looking at society which could live in the same world with others. The rejection of this course and the hardening back on military and other forms of force is justified in the minds of Soviet leaders first by the 'must' of world revolution, and then by the argument that force produces: 'force needs no justification but itself'.

In all that has happened those who have articulated a view of life that they name 'humanism' have played an important role. They have harried the religious, deflated their claims, challenged their beliefs and in the moral sphere produced individuals who have matched their achievements. At present there is much searching discussion of the problem of preserving the human person. In a world which offers so many threats to survival and to freedom there is a convergence of forces to the rescue. It is easy for humanists to see in this a convergence on their own point of view, rather than on the human person. There is a kind of humanist messianism that believes that the future is with their man-centred and anti-religious beliefs and that it is only a matter of time till all religions, whether as organized communities or personally held faiths, collapse into their synthesizing arms. If it is, as I believe, a liberating thing for faith to live with its challengers, this may well be true for humanism also. 'I am not myself satisfied', wrote Bertrand Russell in 1960 'with what I have read or said on the philosophical basis of ethics. I cannot see how to refute the arguments for the subjectivity of ethical values, but I find myself incapable of believing that all that is wrong with wanton cruelty is that I don't like it'. Bertrand Russell implies that he does, or wishes to, believe something more about wanton cruelty and finds too little ground in reasoned, philosophical argument to stand on as a fully moral person. Humanists are men of faith and they usually admit that much to men of religion, from whom they state their main division as being a matter of reasonable versus unreasonable belief. It may turn out in the future that the quarrel between Christians and humanists is 'a quarrel in one house' and that both of them are in a different house from, for example, those who regard man as simply a mechanism or as an object of power.

It is not possible to speak of the contribution of other religions than Christianity to the creation of an international human community in the same terms because they are not parallel organizations: they have not the same world-wide community with its appointed leaders and ways of working together. But their contribution within their own spheres is enormous, and their potential largely unexplored. If there were a more thorough and patient study of them they would tell us things about man that we need to know. One of the things that westerners share is a sharp feeling of individuality, defined largely by that which we are 'over against': therefore we struggle to discover other people and agonize over relationships, over loving and being loved. We are cut off almost entirely from our roots in nature. In an economy judged successful by the amount it produces we use and exhaust material resources, plants and animals. Everything is justified if it is 'for man'. The idea that all life has some fulfilment of its own to attain is alien to most of us.

In Buddhism we would find a radical challenge of some of the most deeply ingrained of our modern ways of thought. The superficial attractions of Buddhism to the modern western intellectual – its agnosticism about the existence of any Absolute and its emphasis on the mind – hide the radical nature of its challenge. That which we cultivate in our civilization, *desire*, whether for goods or achievement or sex, it names as the root of evil. That a man's life is what he can cram into the space between birth and death, that a man *is* his ever-changing body, sensations or personality are equations unacceptable to Buddhist thought. Man walks towards enlightenment, but not what we mean by 'man', not this closely guarded individuality. The residue that a life leaves, that is to say the characteristics that result from thought and discipline provide the continuity of consciousness from life to life, on the way to release from self and its desires. The qualities that such a discipline of the mind induces are unity and peace. Life is holy and avoidance of injury to it the first of the five precepts by which to seek detachment from desire. But a Buddhist is not a moralist living by rules: they are guides to the discovery of the way that each finds for himself.

No doubt every age is impressed by the seriousness of the problems that lie ahead and thinks there is something unique about them. Yet perhaps it is not special pleading to say that the creation of a just international order is something without precedent and of very great inherent difficulty. Where do we go *beyond* protest? The events of 1968 seem to indicate that revolution is not in itself enough: that there must be goals beyond it and that self-discipline is an important factor in the achievement of freedom. In Buddhism, what a man makes of his own life by the discipline of his mind over his actions is closely linked with what he feels about all living things: compassion is what he owes to them because he is part of the same totality of life. The recovery of this sense of wholeness, which represents our own far human origins buried in the origins of life itself, may be vital to our sanity, personal and corporate. How can we possibly impose harmony on the world if we are deeply divided in consciousness between what we have become as the masters of nature and our own lost origins as a part of it? A return to our past is no more possible than a return to the womb, but if we know what we have lost we can begin to recover it by understanding something of what our opposites understand about life and incorporating it into our beliefs.

We know that a moral leap in responsibility has to be made if the knowledge and wealth of the world are to be put at the disposal of its needs and the immense power available to states and to large economic and social units are to serve the cause of justice. The visionary is more our guide than the moralist. We read William Blake, the man whom his contemporaries regarded as a dangerous anarchist, a blasphemer and a madman, and we recognize the seer who prophesied to a rich and hard generation the coming of an order of greater caring for the rejected and the poor. His life seemed to have little influence, but after him came many with an awakened social conscience.

No new field of moral endeavour has guide lines, still less rules. The moral problems of politics are at least as old as the discussion of them in Plato's *Republic* (a staple and acceptable part of the education of the guardians of empire in my lifetime and to one of my present students 'the most revolting book I ever read'). In spite of changes a great deal has remained the same. One could imagine a celestial symposium in which some of the great power-manipulators exchanged their experiences with a good deal of mutual understanding on such enduring topics as dealing with opposition, dropping colleagues, controlling the military, making taxes palatable, politicians' wives, 'the art of the possible'.

But the servant of an international organization would be out of this conversation. He has no power, only what he can win from reluctant governments: far from being his own master, he is the servant of many. He has no party to support him, he cannot 'go to the country'. His court of appeal is the moral conscience of the world – such as it is or can become. Everything has to be made. To Dag Hammarskjöld his work as Secretary-General of the United Nations was one of total moral demand and commitment. His *Markings*, a spiritual diary intermittently kept over a long period and hard to piece into any continuity, show the counterpart of the outward drive to action in the inward pursuit in search of God in the depths of his being and alone. The connection between the two was the occasional fleeting awareness of a divine presence and the continual effort to discipline his mind for the work he had to do. There is nothing here of the feeling of a static moral order sustained and upheld by the authority of God to which he must attempt to conform: one is bound to ask what value such a concept would have been for such a life. A humanist or a Buddhist in such a position as he held, and at such a time as he held it, would have been thrust as he was upon his own inner resources to take his decisions knowing full well that they might have large consequences for the future of the organization he and others were striving to create. We often use the phrase 'man's creativity' in relation to his scientific and artistic achievements. The achievement of new moral insight is also creative achievement. It is not verifiable by success in the present.

Science and technology grew up in a civilization that believed in God. Everybody knows that the fantastic growth of knowledge and power are as nothing compared with the possibilities of further growth in the immediate future. Faced with such powers in man how is it possible to ascribe the term 'Almighty' to any other than man? By these powers the hungry could be fed and much of the misery caused by disease and ignorance could be abolished. An increasing knowledge of the causes of war, genocide, racial antagonism, poverty and many other ills could help to abolish them. If he does not act on such knowledge and such powers, man will have to accept the charge that he levelled at the God he called Almighty, that he could have stopped suffering and would not. With every accretion of man's power therefore the weight of man's moral responsibility and the potentiality of his guilt grows greater. Who will shoulder these responsibilities and will those who do be supported by the active compliance of all in the adjustments and sacrifices that will be the accompaniment of major changes in our habits of thought and life?

Moral achievement takes place when men's conscious aims have the assent of the inner forces that mould their emotional life. Appeals to the will to reinforce moral endeavour are vain if the inner feeling is that what is asked for is impossible. Then there can be a refusal of the demand, a turning away to its opposite. Life for mankind lies in meeting a new moral demand. We see signs of this happening already. But there are also other signs that are far less reassuring. In the constant portrayal of violence and cruelty, the forebodings of racial conflict and the spate of irrational fear let loose by a small incident or a speech one senses a habituation of the mind to opposite courses than those of co-operation for survival and freedom. With the return to contemporary thinking of the myth of the death of god there comes the thought of its meaning: that gods are willed to die when men are to die, for it is intolerable that one should live.

It is not the primary business of religion to reinforce appeals for moral action. All religions are concerned with men's salvation, that means his wholeness. Moral action springs, on any religious view, from alignment of will and emotions towards that whole. There may be fewer who believe in and practise a religious faith but their business is with the response of man's whole being to life. If 'man is the product of causes which had no prevision of the end they were achieving; that his growth, his hopes and fears, his loves and beliefs are but the outcome of an accidental collocation of atoms' . . . if all is doomed to utter extinction including not only man's physical environment but all his achievement, hope and love, if death has totally and finally the last word, then, Bertrand Russell continues in his well-known passage from *A Free Man's Worship* 'only on the firm foundation of unyielding despair, can the soul's habitation henceforth be safely built'. Those words were written when 'unyielding despair' was not a universal attitude. They express the point of view of a dedicated intelligence; but if unyielding despair were to become universal would it offer a firm foundation for a soul's habitation or for the future of mankind?

In face of this no facile reiteration of faith in providential escapes or compensatory rewards is worthy of respect. The moral endeavours of the Buddhist are founded on the faith that there is an Enlightenment to be achieved, that an already enlightened one has pointed the way. For Jews, Christians and Moslems the meaning of life is found not in the thrust of power that set the universe on its chance-originated way, but in the end towards which all life is called and drawn. In the marvellous fresco of Michelangelo the waking figure of Adam rises struggling from the dust, touched by the finger of God. The futile efforts to make of the profound insight of the Genesis story the first event of history hide its real meaning, which is not that man *was* created but that he *is*, by a creator timelessly present to all time. Released from the responsibility of being God, man is free to be himself, free not as a tool or an agent but as one who can create and also sin.

Christianity, most vulnerable of these historic faiths, does not claim that it is itself completed. 'Christian faith constantly rises on the ground of the conquest of unbelief which it has always at its side to vex it.'[1] That is its vocation today. Its central doctrines are not for assent but for testing: resurrection has no meaning if man does not find new life: the historic revelation was no revelation if death is triumphant. But in the 'not yet' of hope, not the 'already decided' of despair, the man of faith, if he is really such, works for man's fulfilment.

[1] MOLTMANN. *Theology of Hope.*

BIBLIOGRAPHY

GENERAL

BROTHERS, JOAN (ed.), *Readings in the Sociology of Religion* (Pergamon, 1965).

DAVIES, RUPERT, *Religious Authority in an Age of Doubt* (Epworth, 1968).

DEWART, D. L., *The Future of Belief* (Burns, Oates, 1967).

EVANS-PRITCHARD, E. E., *Theories of Primitive Religion* (O.U.P., 1965).

HERBERG, WILL, *Protestant, Catholic, Jew* (Anchor Books, 1960).

HUXLEY, JULIAN, *Religion without Revelation* (Watts, 1967).

KIERKEGAARD, *Selections introduced by W. H. Auden* (Cassell, 1955).

KRAEMER, H., *Religion and the Christian Faith* (Lutterworth, 1958).

LEWIS, H. D. & SLATER, R. L., *World Religions* (Watts, 1966).

MOORMAN, J., *Vatican II* (Darton, Longman & Todd, 1967).

OTTO, R., *The Idea of the Holy* (O.U.P., 1923).

PAUL, LESLIE, *Alternatives to Christian Belief* (Hodder & Stoughton, 1967).

SMITH, WILFRED CANTWELL, *The Meaning and End of Religion* (Mentor Books, 1962).

TAYLOR, JOHN, *The Primal Vision* (S.C.M.).

VATICAN II, *Documents of* (Chapman, 1967).

WACH, J., *The Comparative Study of Religion* (Chicago 1944, University Press).

YINGER, J. MILTON, *Religion, Society and the Individual* (Macmillan, 1957).

ZAEHNER, R. C. (ed.), *The Concise Encyclopedia of Living Faiths.*

BUILDINGS

BIRMINGHAM Institute for the Study of Worship and Religious Architecture, *Buildings and Breakthrough.*

CATT, JOHN, *Church Building* (three times a year).

DAVIES, HORTON, *Worship and Theology in England, 1690–1850*.

DAVIES, J. G., *The Secular Use of Church Buildings* (S.C.M., 1968).

HAMMOND, PETER, *Liturgy and Architecture* (S.C.M.).

LUDOWYK, E. F. C., *The Footprint of the Buddha* (Allen & Unwin, 1958).

VERNEY, STEPHEN, *Fire in Coventry* (Hodder & Stoughton, 1964).

PROFESSIONALS

Non-Christian

CRAGG, KENNETH, *The Call of the Minaret* (O.U.P., 1956).

DUTT, SUKUMUR, *Buddhist Monks and Monasteries* (Allen & Unwin, 1962).

EPSTEIN, ISIDORE, *Judaism* (Penguin, 1959).

HUMPHRIES, CHRISTMAS, *Buddhism* (Pelican, 3rd edn., 1962).

NAIR, BALAKRISHNA, *The Dynamic Brahmins* (Popular Pr., Bombay, 1968).

THICH NHAT HANH, *The Lotus in the Sea of Fire* (S.C.M., 1967).

WRIGHT, ARTHUR, *Buddhism in Chinese History* (Stanford University).

ZAEHNER, R. C., *Hinduism* (Pelican).

Christian

BAINTON, *Yale and the Ministry* (Yale University).

CHADWICK, OWEN, *The Victorian Church* (A. & C. Black, 1966).

DAVIS, CHARLES, *A Question of Conscience* (Hodder & Stoughton, 1967).

DE FOUCAULD, CHARLES, *Spiritual Biography* (New York: P. J. Kennedy & Sons, 1964).

FICHTER, JOSEPH H., *Religion as an Occupation* (University of Chicago).

HARRISON, PAUL M., *Authority and Power in the Free Church Tradition* (Princeton University, 1959).

NEILL, S., *Anglicanism* (Pelican, 3rd edn., 1965).

PAUL, LESLIE, *The Deployment and Payment of the Clergy* (Church Inf. Office, 1964).

PUSEY, N., *The Episcopal Ministry* (New York, 1967).

WHYTE, WILLIAM, *The Organization Man* (New York: Simon & Schuster, 1956).

ADHERENTS

ARGYLE, M., *Religious Behaviour* (Routledge & Kegan Paul, 1958).

BRANDON, OWEN, *Christianity from Within* (Hodder & Stoughton, 1965).

BUSIA, K., *Urban Churches in Britain* (Lutterworth, 1966).

COULSON, JOHN (ed.), *Theology and the University* (Darton, Longman & Todd, 1964).

CRAGG, K., *Christianity and World View* (O.U.P., 1968).

DAVIES, HORTON. *The English Free Church Tradition* (O.U.P. 1951).

EPSTEIN, ISIDORE, *Judaism* (Penguin, 1959).

JAMES, WILLIAM, *The Varieties of Religious Experience* (Longmans, 1902).

KRAEMER, H., *Christianity and World Religions.*

MARRIS, P., *The Experience of Higher Education* (Routledge, 1964).

MEAD, MARGARET, *Male and Female* (Penguin, 1962).

PAYNE, ERNEST, *The Free Church Tradition in the Life of England* (Hodder & Stoughton, 1962).

PICKERING, W. S. F., 'Religious Movements of Church Members in Two Working-Class Towns in England' (*Archives de Sociol. des Religions* II, 1961).

PURDY, W., *The Church on the Move* (Holles & Carter).

REEVES, M., *Eighteen plus* (Faber, 1965).

SARGENT, W., *Battle for the Mind* (Heinemann, 1957).

WILLIAMS, COLIN W., *Where in the World?* (Epworth, 1963).

WORLD Council of Churches, *The Missionary structure of the Congregation.*

RELIGION IN THE SCHOOLS

ALVES, C., *Religion and the Secondary School* (S.C.M., 1958).

BECK, ARCHBISHOP, in: *Looking forward to the 70's* (ed. Peter Bander) (Pan, 1959).

BLISS, K. (ed.), *Education and the Nature of Man* (World Council of Churches).

Cox, E., *Sixth Form Religion* (S.C.M., 1967).

Goldman, R., *Religious Thinking from Childhood to Adolescence* (Routledge, 1965).

Hyde, K. E., *Religious Learning in Adolescence* (University of Birmingham, 1965).

Loukes, Harold, *Teenage Religion* (S.C.M. Press).

Jungman, G. V., *Handing on the Faith* (Burns Oates, 1959).

Lewis, E., *Children and their Religion* (Sheed & Ward, 1962).

JESUS

Baillie, D. M., *God was in Christ*.

Bartsch, H. W. (ed.), *Kerygma and Myth – a Theological Debate* (S.P.C.K., 1962).

Bornkamm, G., *Jesus of Nazareth* (Hodder & Stoughton, 1963).

Buber, Martin, *I and Thou* (T. & T. Clarke, 1939).

Bultmann, R., *Jesus Christ and Mythology* (S.C.M., 1960).

Burrows, M., *The Dead Sea Scrolls*.

Jenkins, David, *The Glory of Man* (S.C.M., 1968).

Lanternari, V., *Religions of the Oppressed* (Mentor Books, 1965).

Mâle, Emile, *The Gothic Image* (Fontana, 1961).

Mirgeler, Albert, *Mutations of Western Christianity*.

Neill, S., *The Interpretations of the New Testament 1861–1961* (O.U.P.).

Smart, Ninian, *World Religions: A Dialogue* (Penguin, 1966).

Sundkler, Bengt, *Bantu Prophets* (O.U.P. paperback).

Van Peursen, C. A., *Body, Soul and Spirit: a survey of the body–mind problem* (Oxford, 1967).

Weil, Simone, *Waiting on God* (Routledge, 1951; Fontana, 1959).

GOD

Baeltz, Peter, *Prayer and Providence* (S.C.M., 1968).

Baillie, John, *Our Knowledge of God* (Pelican).

Berdyaev, N., *Freedom of the Spirit* (Geoffrey Books, 1935).

Bosanquet, Mary, *The Life and Death of Dietrich Bonhoeffer* (Hodder & Stoughton, 1968).

De Lubac, H., *Le phenomène de l'humanisme athée* (Ed. Spes., Paris, 1945).

De Lubac, H., *The Discovery of God* (Darton, Longman & Todd, 1960).

Hodgson, Leonard, *The Place of Reason in Christian Apologetics* (O.U.P., 1925).

Hodgson, Leonard, *For Faith and Freedom* (S.C.M., 1968).

Koch, Hans-Gerhard, *The Abolition of God* (S.C.M., 1963).

Ramsey, Ian T., *Religious Language* (S.C.M., 1957).

Robinson, John, *Exploration into God* (S.C.M., 1967).

Tillich, Paul, *Systematic Theology, Vol.* I (Nisbet, 1953).

Tillich, Paul, *Biblical Religion and the Search for Ultimate Reality* (Nisbet, 1955).

Woods, G. F., *Theological Explanation* (Nisbet, 1955).

INDEX

MORE ABOUT PENGUINS
AND PELICANS

Penguinews, which appears every month, contains details of all the new books issued by Penguins as they are published. From time to time it is supplemented by *Penguins in Print*, which is a complete list of all available books published by Penguins. (There are well over three thousand of these.)

A specimen copy of *Penguinews* will be sent to you free on request, and you can become a subscriber for the price of the postage. For a year's issues (including the complete lists) please send 30p if you live in the United Kingdom, or 60p if you live elsewhere. Just write to Dept EP, Penguin Books Ltd, Harmondsworth, Middlesex, enclosing a cheque or postal order, and your name will be added to the mailing list.

Note: *Penguinews* and *Penguins in Print* are not available in the U.S.A. or Canada

THE STUDY OF RELIGIONS

H. D. Lewis and Robert Lawson Slater

'To maintain that all religions are paths leading to the same goal, as is so frequently done today, is to maintain something that is not true. Not only on the dogmatic, but on the mystical plane, too, there is no agreement.'

These downright words from an expert on oriental religion reflect the modern, realistic approach to the comparative study of religions. The results of western re-appraisal of three great living traditions – Hinduism, Buddhism, and Islam – are outlined in the first part of this Pelican by Professor Slater, who discusses the history, literature, beliefs and practices of these religions and comments on their internal diversity and their attitudes to divinity. In the second part Professor H. D. Lewis relates trends in philosophy to the study of religions, examines the Hindu and Buddhist concepts of God, and questions whether such Christians as Paul Tillich have done well, in the high-minded cause of fraternity, to generalize their faith to the point at which it loses its essential Christianity. This book was originally published under the title *World Religions*.